What You Want To Know About
BUDGERIGARS

What You Want To Know About BUDGERIGARS

Eric L. Johns

Robert Hale Limited
London

© *Eric L. Johns 1971, 1975, 1978, 1979 and 1982*

First published in Great Britain 1971

Second Edition 1975

Reprinted 1975

Third Edition 1978

Reprinted 1979

Reprinted 1982

ISBN 0 7091 7058 0

Robert Hale Limited
Clerkenwell House
Clerkenwell Green
London EC1R OHT

PRINTED IN GREAT BRITAIN BY
CLARKE, DOBLE & BRENDON
PLYMOUTH AND BOUND BY
WESTERN BOOK

CONTENTS

	Foreword	9
	Introduction	10
1	Buying a Pet Budgie	11
2	A Budgerigar's Requirements	18
3	Your Bird's Perches	24
4	Training your Budgie to Talk	29
5	Breeding	32
6	The History of the Budgie	40
7	Colours in Budgies and how to Breed them	43
8	Your Questions Answered	50
9	Ailments and Injuries	78
10	The Budgie as a Healer of the Sick	102
11	Why I Love the Budgie	105
12	The Budgerigar Society and Further Books on the Budgerigar	109
	Index	119

ILLUSTRATIONS

facing page

A fine collection of budgies in an outdoor aviary 14

A six-week old budgie, hand tame on the author's finger 15

A pet bird in the new type of modern cage, which gives the bird plenty of room to move 15

Seeding grass and chickweed, the finest natural tonics available for budgies 30

Plain matchstick for giving powder to budgies; burnt matchstick for ringing chicks; tweezers useful for several purposes; plier-type clippers for trimming claws and beaks; medicine dropper; nail trimmers for cutting small areas of claws that have become split or broken 30

The standard budgerigar show cage 31

A travelling case for show cages 31

The Budgerigar Society's ideal budgerigar 46

An exhibition light-green normal cock 46

Three different varieties of budgies 47

The albino, which has red eyes and a clear white body 47

Between pages 62 *and* 63

Two types of nest-boxes

Breeding pairs in cages and nest-boxes

The first four eggs out of seven

The first one out. A budgie chick of less than twelve hours old

The first chick is now seven days old and has company

Four chicks

The chicks at the ages of twenty-four, twenty-two, twenty and eighteen days old and beginning to get their proper feathers

The oldest of the chicks is now five weeks old

facing page

A budgie being given medicine with a dropper 78

A budgie's claws being trimmed 78

A spacious outside flight 79

LINE DRAWINGS

pages

Perches: the right and wrong sort 25

Cages 26 and 27

Ringing a chick 54

Principal points of a budgerigar 75

FOREWORD

Mr. Eric Johns has made a lifetime study of budgerigars, and this has meant more than just breeding fine specimens for shows at which he has had considerable success. He has an unusual understanding of these birds as he has demonstrated in this book.

Mr. Johns knows how to train budgerigars to speak and so has proved their especial value as companions for the housebound or the elderly.

This book should prove of interest to all bird fanciers and to those who are just looking for an attractive companion or pet.

Joan Vickers
(Dame of the British Empire)

INTRODUCTION

Many books have been written on the welfare of the fascinating budgie, but I make no apology for including this book amongst them. The number of people who keep these birds is phenomenal; and I know from my own experience that such is the popularity of the budgie that each day many thousands find themselves in new homes. It is for the new owner, and for those who know little of the budgerigar and the aspects of the Fancy associated with them, that I have written this book.

Therefore if anyone, having read it, finds it helpful in keeping his birds fit, and at the same time it gives them an insight into the wonderful budgerigar Fancy as a whole, I will then know that I have succeeded in my purpose.

To conclude I would like to express my sincere appreciation to the secretary and officials of the Budgerigar Society for allowing me to reproduce the model of their Ideal Budgerigar, the Standard Show Cage and other Budgerigar Society details.

Eric L. Johns

ONE

Buying a Pet Budgie

As it is most likely that this book will be read by many who have yet to buy their first budgie, I feel it appropriate to commence by giving some hints and answering the questions that prospective buyers of pet budgies ask.

First then, at what age should a pet budgie be obtained?

The best time to purchase a budgie that you hope will eventually talk, is as soon as it leaves its parents and is capable of feeding itself—this is usually at 6 to 7 weeks. If you can obtain one of this age you have every advantage as it is at this time that young budgies have very little fear of humans, and is therefore easy to hand tame. With care and patience you should be able to put your hand in the cage and get the budgie to come onto your fingers within a few days of obtaining it; but if you should find that your pet does not do this, do not keep putting your hand up to the bird, but just rest your fingers on the perch when the bird is on it. If you have the time (it might take perhaps ten minutes the first couple of occasions), and it is essential that you really allow your finger to rest on the perch quite still, with the patience to do this you will find that the bird will eventually come on to your finger. By persevering you will have made a start towards gaining the bird's confidence. Once this is achieved, you will soon have the greatest and the most amusing pet you have ever had; but it is better to start with a young bird since comparatively few adult birds respond well to such training.

As most of the people who wish to buy a budgie as a pet hope that eventually the bird they purchase will talk, it is natural that they want to know which will make the best talkers—cock (male) or hen budgies, and how they can tell the difference in the sexes.

As this is a two-part question, I will begin by answering the first part. There are hen birds that talk as well as cock birds, but I think there are far more cock birds that are fluent talkers. So, personally, if I was buying a pet budgie in the hope that it would talk, I would obtain a male. However, both cocks and hens can be wonderful pets, and talking is only one of the many virtues of these captivating creatures. Even if they do not have loquacious ability, they are usually so amusing and entertaining that I don't think their lack of speech is so very important. One that can do tricks and play games (most can) is equally amusing, but such is the talent of the budgie that many can do the lot!

Now to the second part of the question—how can we tell the sex of the budgie?

To help us here we must look at the colour of the cere or wattle, this is the bony piece which goes across the top of the beak. In a cock bird the cere should be blue (except in lutinos and albinos when it is a pinky shade), and in hens it should be brown.

In mature birds it is usually easy to see which is which, but when budgies first leave the nest it is not always so easy! Most experienced breeders can normally tell the sex of the bird at about six weeks, but even the most expert can be wrong at times. The reason for this is that often young hen birds have a pale blue cere, and at so young an age they can be mistaken for cock birds. It is only after they have completed their first moult that the cere colour changes to the customary brown. This often accounts for many being sold by inexperienced fanciers as cock birds, which are later found to be hens.

The ceres of young cocks often have a pinky look about them, and if this is the case the pink of the cere has a 'solid' definite shade, whereas young hens which happen to have pale blue ceres often have a touch of white in the blue. Close observation will show these minute white specks (that's all they are) around the nostril holes in the cere; these are a definite indication that the bird is a hen. When I have seen these small white patches on the cere, even if the rest of the cere is blue, I have never known the bird to be anything but a female; but often it is only the expert who can observe these white patches. Young cock birds which sometimes have pinky-coloured ceres remain like this until they begin to moult, when the cere then changes to blue. So you can see that sexing young budgies can be difficult at times, even to the experienced.

The potential buyer often asks, "What should I look for when I am purchasing a bird?"

First see that the bird you are thinking of buying has all its feathers in the wings and tail. Although it is not a common complaint, budgies can sometimes be born with what is known as French moult. This is a feather condition which affects the wings and tail. The feathers begin to grow on the wings and tail and then break off, so that the affected bird cannot fly and becomes what is known as a 'runner'. Despite the fact that thousands of people are interested in French moult no one has yet been able to find the definite cause of this feather disorder. Fortunately there are not many birds bred with this complaint; but should you see one of the birds for sale do not buy it, as often the feathers on the wings and tail never grow properly, and so you will have a pet that will never be able to fly.

Usually these birds with French moult find a good home, but if they are to be kept as pets it is better for two or three of them to be kept together. One year a friend of mine bred three of these 'runners' amongst more than 100 perfectly healthy youngsters. He was quite concerned about these three birds, which were very tame and friendly, and did not like to destroy them. He found a home for them when a young orphan girl came to see him and asked if he could let her have a pet bird cheap for her invalid aunt. My friend explained that he had these three 'runners' and she could have one or the three of them for nothing, upon which she went away very excited. In a few minutes she was back again to say that Auntie would have all three, and so my friend was happy to find a good home for these unfortunate birds. Later I heard that, although they had never grown their feathers on the wings and tail and were still 'runners', they could do a variety of tricks, and had made the invalid aunt a very happy person as they were always "up to something".

People are always asking questions concerning talking budgies. A typical query is, "Which colour budgie makes the best talker?"

I often smile to myself when I am asked this—as how can feather colour define which bird will talk the best? Take colour of hair in human beings for example. Does a fair-haired child always talk more than a dark-haired one? You know the answer, and it is the same with budgies; and yet some people are certain that only budgies of a particular colour will talk. This is pure nonsense. To prove my point, just before I began to write this I had two people to see me. They had come separately, but both

A fine collection of budgies in an outdoor aviary. The predominately white ones are Danish recessive pieds

A six-week old budgie, hand tame on the author's finger. This bird is now a fluent talker

A pet bird in the new type of modern cage, which gives the bird plenty of room to move

wanted a young budgie that would talk. The first lady was very definite in her views: "I must have a green one, blues are never any good. All the green budgies I have had have talked, and the reason for this is because the first wild budgies were green in colour." The second lady also had a firm opinion: "It must be blue. I have had green budgies, but you never get a word out of them. Yes, it must be a blue—they are natural talkers!"

So you see how people vary in their opinions. Both these ladies sincerely believed that only the particular colour they favoured talked, yet how could they both be right? By coincidence they found that when they bought a certain coloured budgie it talked, so they assumed that only that particular colour had loquacious talent, and yet if either of these people had bought a yellow, or a white or any other coloured budgie for that matter, they would probably have found that one of these could have been trained to talk as fluently as a green or blue one.

I am sure that colour has nothing to do with a budgie's gift for talking. I have heard numerous budgies of various colours speaking fluently. Colour should not influence your decision in your quest for one that would talk; but if you choose the colour you like, it will make you happy and give you a feeling that it is the 'best' bird for you!

Whilst on the subject of buying a budgie, often in the papers you see budgies advertised as a "talking strain". Whilst it is probably quite true that these were bred from a family that produced talkers, there is no such thing as a 'strain' of budgies which are guaranteed to talk. As I said previously when discussing certain colours which are supposed to talk better than others, it is pure chance. You could buy a blue one which might never utter a word, whereas another blue one might be a talking 'wonder';

and so it is with 'talking strain' budgies—some might be fluent talkers and others have little or no vocal talent.

Previously I mentioned that I had heard numerous budgies talking, and amongst these were two which were really remarkable, not only for what they said, but also for the clarity of their speech. Both of these had come from parents which were exhibition specimens. Although I have never bred budgies for talking, I have always been interested in exhibiting them, and several which I have let people have as pets have turned out to be very good speakers; so please don't think it particularly necessary to give a high price for a budgie from a 'talking strain'. Providing it is young enough and you have the patience to teach it, every budgie is a potential talker.

To assist those of you who would like some suggestions on how to train a budgie to talk, I am going to write about this later in the book. During the last twelve months my family and I have kept a pet budgie in the house. Previously I had always kept my birds in an aviary in the garden, but our pet Georgie is now one of the family, and with tuition from my family is becoming a fluent talker. I will tell you later how we trained him.

On the subject of buying a budgie, here is a word of warning. If you go to a budgie breeder for a young one, and you see the one you like, but the breeder says "I'm not sure if it's eating yet, as it's only been out of the nest a day or so," don't take it home right away, but ask the fancier to keep the bird for a few days more to be sure it can look after itself. If you wish to make certain that the bird will not be sold to someone else, a small deposit can be given to the breeder.

I mention this as it is very important that you do not obtain a pet too young to eat, as nothing is more depressing than to have a bird which cannot do this. Often in this case it will die, and as no one wishes this to happen, it is wise to make sure that the bird is old enough before bringing it home.

Now, assuming you have just bought a budgie, I am going to suggest how you can help it for the first day or so that it is in its new cage. Often youngsters will die if taken from their parents before they can eat properly, but young birds also sometimes die because they are put in new cages where they feel strange or frightened for the first day or so. They sometimes cannot find or understand where the seed and water is, and so starve, their new owners not realizing this until it is too late.

So when you bring home your new 'pal', besides seeing that the seed and water containers are full, also put a dish of water and some seed in the bottom of the cage. By doing this you will be ensuring that the bird will have immediate access to its food. Once you have seen it eat and drink from the proper troughs, you need not put the water or seed on the bottom of the cage, but until you are sure, it is better to be safe than sorry!

TWO

A Budgerigar's Requirements

In the last chapter I gave some hints to those who were anticipating buying a budgie, in this chapter I am going to mention the necessities for a budgie's welfare. I hope these remarks will help those of you who have just acquired a pet, and also those who have kept a bird for some time and who would like further information about the needs of the fascinating little budgie.

Due to my interest in birds, I often speak to people who keep pet birds, and it surprises and saddens me that so many owners, through sheer lack of knowledge, often think that the only requirements of their feathered friend are a little canary seed and water.

It is true that this will keep a bird alive! But the aim of anyone who keeps pets (whether it is birds or animals) should be to keep them healthy and happy. We should remember that good health helps to make a bird happy, so it is appropriate that we should understand the necessities for a bird's nourishment.

WATER

Fresh water should be given daily, and so that it should be at its best, the drinker or water container should be thoroughly washed under the tap at least every other day, as it is surprising how grimy these can get if not cleaned regularly.

SEED

The main diet of budgies in cages or aviaries is canary seed and millet seed (there are several varieties of these), and if you keep one or a small number of birds I do not think you can do better than buy seed which is already mixed with the right proportion of various canary and millet seeds.

I will mention more about seed in a moment, but would like first to propose how you should fill the seed container.

I am referring to this as several times I have had urgent requests to "call and have a look at Joey (for some reason almost every pet bird I have known has been called Joey), as he seems a bit mopey and isn't eating much seed." I go around to see the 'feathered friend' who is causing so much anxiety through not eating, and on almost every occasion the look of the bird is the same. Although not looking in really glowing health, he doesn't look very bad. He seems fairly active, and when he remains still I notice that his tail does not move. When a bird isn't well it usually finds breathing difficult, and with its heavier breathing its tail will flick up and down incessantly. When a bird's tail moves like this (unless it has become frightened, which will make the tail act like this for a short while until the bird calms down) it is usually an indication that something is wrong. But with the bird I am discussing there is no tail flicking and no symptoms of bowel trouble, the bird's droppings being normal black and white in appearance.

Here is a mystery. A budgie reasonably well, although not its radiant self, but not eating as much seed as it should. Looking in the cage I find there is grit and cuttle-fish bone, so there is no alternative but to examine the seed in the pot. I take this out of the cage and tip the seed from the pot on to some paper spread on the table, and the 'mystery' is solved! The reason that an apparently healthy bird is not eating much seed is because there is not much seed to eat!

Each day the owners' of the birds concerned had taken the seed-pot from the cage, noticed a few empty seed husks on the top of the seed, blown this into a bin, and put some new seed on the top of the old. This principle of feeding is all right if you feed your bird twice daily, and once a week throw all the seed in the pot away and refill with completely fresh seed. But in the case of the bird which I have referred to this was not done, the empty seed was blown off the top for indefinite periods, and so just below the fresh seed was old seed, empty seed husks and seed dust that had accumulated over the weeks. The result was that in each case the bird could not 'stomach' most of the 'seed' in the pot, had gone on a partial 'hunger strike' and was virtually starving. When I explained the reason for the bird's lack of appetite, the owners were shocked, but took my advice and threw the 'seed' in the pot away, and, what is equally important, gave the seed-pot a good rinse out. Then, after thoroughly drying it, they filled it with fresh seed, and I am pleased to say that in a few days the bird was once more its healthy, hungry self.

Perhaps you feel I have written a lot about such a matter? But ample, fresh, clean seed is the first basic necessity for your birds' welfare.

Besides mixed seed for your budgerigar, there is a seed tit-bit which could be given two or three times a week. This is millet spray, which is millet seed still on the stalk as it was grown. Very few budgies can resist this, and besides eating the seed which is very beneficial, the bird will get a thrill from biting at the stalk, usually doing this until it is in threads.

If those of you reading this book have budgies which are breeding and wish to give them something additional in the way of food I suggest a small amount of groats or oats daily. These varieties of corn are still reasonable in price and are an excellent food supplement for breeding budgies when they have youngsters. I have not advised feeding groats or oats to pet budgies as unfortunately they are inclined to make birds fat, and this is one of the worst things a pet can be.

GRIT

Grit is another item which is as important for a bird's welfare as food and water. Although it is absolutely essential, it is a sad fact that there are numerous budgies which, I am certain, have never seen grit, let alone eaten it!

Having said grit is so important I would like to explain why.

Birds do not have teeth and so grit (which is tiny pieces of stone or minerals, specially prepared for birds) takes the place of teeth in a bird.

When the grit is swallowed, it goes into the bird's gizzard, and remains there until it has worn so small that it eventually passes through the bowels of the bird. During the time that the grit is in the gizzard it helps to cut up the seed that is swallowed, and so assists the bird to masticate and digest its food properly. Therefore you can see how essential it is that your pet should have a constant supply of grit available, as without this being replenished regularly it is likely to suffer from digestive troubles. So always have a small pot of grit in the bottom of the cage and avoid this trouble.

CUTTLE-FISH BONE

That white bone which can be bought at pet stores is known as cuttle-fish bone, and this should always be available as it provides calcium and also helps to keep your bird's beak in order. A word of caution, however. Should you ever find this cuttle-fish bone on the beach, make certain that it does not have any oil or oil-stains on it. If there is any doubt whether the bone is really oil-free, please don't use it! It is much better to pay a few pence and buy some. Most birds will eagerly bite at the cuttle-fish bone; but like all living creatures, there is always the exception! So should your bird ignore the bone when it is hung in the cage, just gently scrape a knife over the soft part of the bone. This will produce a powder which can be put in the bottom of the cage, and will in all probability soon be eaten up.

EXTRAS

So far I have dealt with the main essentials for a pet budgie's diet, and now we come to the extras and tit-bits that a bird can be given and which will be enjoyed without causing any upset to the bird (as some tit-bits do).

The extras I quote are some that I have found to be beneficial with my own birds. I mention this because since I have had birds I have spoken to hundreds of people who have kept pet birds, and it is truly fantastic what some people give their birds—it is even more surprising that their birds live, often to an old age. Nevertheless, although I have heard of many birds which have been given many sorts of extras and have lived, I still think it wrong that budgies should be given anything that is not natural and easily digestible. It should be remembered that the budgie in its natural state has a basic diet of seeding grasses; therefore to give a pet budgie all sorts of liquids and foods which are suitable for human beings, although this is done with good intentions, is thoughtless and sometimes cruel! Having said this I will now mention some extras which my birds enjoy.

The budgerigar when in the wild looks upon grass as its main source of food, and I have found that budgies in a cage or aviary still look upon this as a delicacy, and enjoy almost every kind of grass, one of the most liked being the ordinary lawn variety.

At certain times of the year the grasses ripen, and the seeding heads are eagerly eaten. When there is seeding grass I give my birds a little nearly every day. When there are only plain grass leaves, this and bits of the root are equally enjoyed by my birds and I have found this to be a good tonic for them. I would suggest you give your bird some plain grass twice a week when seeding grass is not available.

Be certain when giving your bird grass (or any other green-food for that matter) that it is thoroughly clean—by that I mean free from animal-fouling, weed-killer and frost.

Other extras that most budgies will enjoy are lettuce, cabbage, perpetual spinach and that wonderful weed that every budgie loves—chickweed.

It is better to give green food to your bird early in the day, and to remove it when it is crumpled or stale later.

If it is frosty weather take no chances with outdoor green food, but give your 'pal' a piece of apple which he or she should eat with delight.

THREE

Your Bird's Perches

One of the most important things for birds kept in cages are their perches, and yet this is often never realized by their owners and birds suffer discomfort which could be avoided.

To a bird a perch is as important as a chair to you, and I know that if you found a chair that was uncomfortable you would move to another one. As a bird cannot always do this, it is up to us to see that our pets have comfortable perches, so I am going to give some hints that will help you to do this.

Perches can never be too clean, but they should never be polished to make them shiny. I have seen perches so smooth with being cleaned and rubbed that they were almost shining. Perches like this are nice to look at, but very unpleasant to the birds using them, as when they are so smooth they are very slippery and the birds find it difficult to grip the perch firmly. Smooth perches often cause birds to have corns and callouses, which can be very painful, so always see that your bird's perches are not too smooth. A way to avoid them becoming too shiny is to rub them gently over with a file. This will not make them really rough, but just enough for the bird to get a steady grip on them.

A budgie can also be uncomfortable if the perches are

placed wrongly. Nearly all birds prefer to use the highest perch in the cage, and frequently I see cages with one of the perches almost at the top of the cage—so near the top in fact, that when the bird is on this perch (which it nearly always is!) it can only stay there by bending over. Just imagine how unpleasant this must be for it. If this perch were lowered, the bird would be able to stand upright, and also could jump up on it more easily—which would make the occupant more lively and healthy.

On the left are unsuitable perches: *(top)* too small, *(centre)* too large, *(bottom)* square with sharp corners. On the right is the correct type of perch.

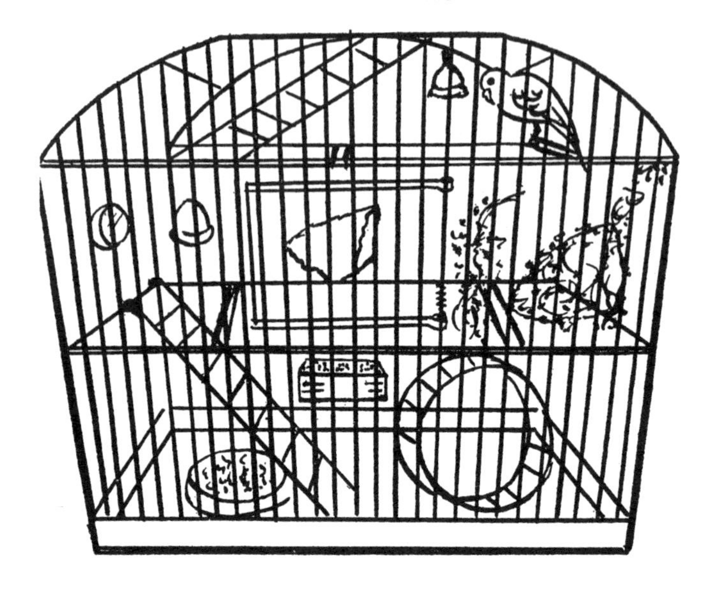

Now, about the number of perches required.

There are some beautiful cages in the shops, but unfortunately some of these have not sufficient perches. At the bottom they have a perch each end so that the bird can reach the seed and water troughs, which is quite right. But then for some obscure reason, there is often one long perch which goes right through the middle of the cage from end to end. Although this looks nice, it isn't so nice for the bird, because the absence of a second perch in the top half of the cage means that it cannot jump from perch to perch, and when it does fly off the perch for exercise it has to turn and twist itself to get on to it again. This to me is a bad thing. If you have these long single perches in your bird's cage, I would suggest that you take this perch out, cut it small enough to fix from one side of the cage to the other, and put it at one

(left) An overcrowded cage with badly-placed perches. *(above)* There is room for the budgie to move in this cage.

end. Then obtain another piece of wood suitable for a perch and cut and fix it to the other end of the cage, so that there is a perch each end. When you have done this, your pet will soon let you see its pleasure now that it can jump from side to side.

I have mentioned that it is wrong not to have sufficient perches, but it is even worse to have too many perches and other oddments in a cage, which prevents the occupant from being able to move freely. There should be space between the perches for a pet to be able to flap its wings should it want to.

Whilst I am on the subject of perches, there are perhaps some of you wondering where you can obtain wood suitable for bird perching. Some pet stores sell the appropriate size perching, but you can also obtain dowel rods from ironmongers or do-it-yourself stores. These rods can be bought in various lengths and thicknesses, the ideal thickness for budgies being $\frac{5}{8}$-inch perches. Should you buy these and find them very smooth and shiny, rub a file gently over them as previously mentioned, before inserting them in the cage.

Natural perching is even better than dowelling as not only do these vary in size—which is good for the bird's feet—but also the bird can bite and strip the natural bark off the branch, which is good for its health. If you use twigs as perches they will have to be renewed from time to time, due to the bird constantly biting them. I have found the twigs of apple and pear trees to be ideal for budgies.

FOUR

Training your Budgie to Talk

Our first aim in teaching a budgie to talk should be to gain the bird's complete confidence. This can usually be achieved initially by talking to it as often as you can. Even one or two words spoken as you pass the cage from time to time will help your pet to feel at ease with you.

Having done this, you should then put your hand in the cage for a few minutes each day, gently resting it on the perch near your pet, without touching him or her. After doing this a few times it will realize that you are not going to harm it, and in due course should come to your hand. Your trust is essential in the training of your pet, as timid nervous budgies are very unlikely to become talkers.

With young budgies (just like children) the first attempts at speaking are queer twitterings. Although they are uttering strange sounds, what these are will remain a 'mystery' for a few weeks, but it is at this stage that we should start our bird on its basic training. Here again a young budgie is like a young child; if it is to be taught to speak, it must be given short, simple words to learn, one word to start with being repeated over and over again until your pet can say it. Even when it can say this word continue to repeat it until he or she can say it very distinctly. Don't be in a hurry to teach your pet a lot of words. If this is done the bird will probably be a poor speaker, chattering away in the normal budgie manner and occasionally uttering a human word. This is all right in a way, but if our wish is to have a pet that talks it is better that it should talk clearly and often.

So you should remember to teach your pet slowly and (I hope) surely, as one word spoken clearly will give more pleasure to an owner than twenty words which can't be really understood.

Now, assuming your pet can say one word properly, you should now go further and join other words on to it. If the first word you teach your pet is its name—Joey, for instance—you can now add the word "pretty", and so keep repeating "Pretty Joey". Once he or she has learnt to say the first word it should be quite capable of learning this new word in a week or so; and once it has really acquired the gift of speech, it will often add words to its repertoire without tuition.

To quote an instance of this, when the pet budgie we now have was about twelve weeks' old it could speak one word fluently, its name, Georgie. About this time I took my family away for a few days holiday and Georgie was looked after by my mother, who years ago had a bird named Joey. Whilst we were away she absent-mindedly called him Joey at times, and when we arrived back we found that our pet instead of saying, "Georgie" was saying, "Georgie Joey"—which illustrates how quickly budgies can pick-up new words once they can talk.

What is wonderful about the talking budgie is not only the wide range of words he or she is quite capable of using, but also the way it imitates the sound of the voice of whoever teaches it. Some have the high-pitched voice of their lady owner, whilst others have deeper masculine voices denoting they have a male tutor.

Seeding grass and chickweed, the finest natural tonics available for budgies

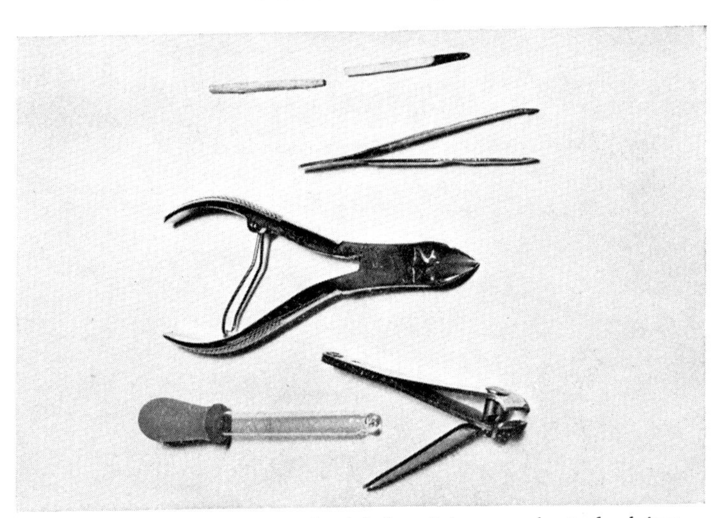

Top to bottom: plain matchstick for giving powder to budgies; burnt matchstick for ringing chicks; tweezers useful for several purposes; plier-type clippers for trimming claws and beaks; medicine dropper; nail trimmers for cutting small areas of claws that have become split or broken

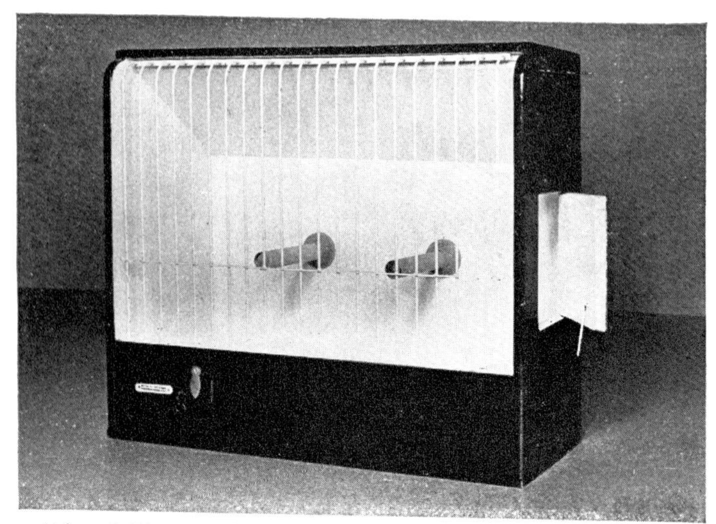

(Above) The standard budgerigar show cage (reproduced by courtesy of the Budgerigar Society). *(Below)* A travelling case for show cages. Seed is on the bottom of the cages; front ventilation holes can be closed in cold weather

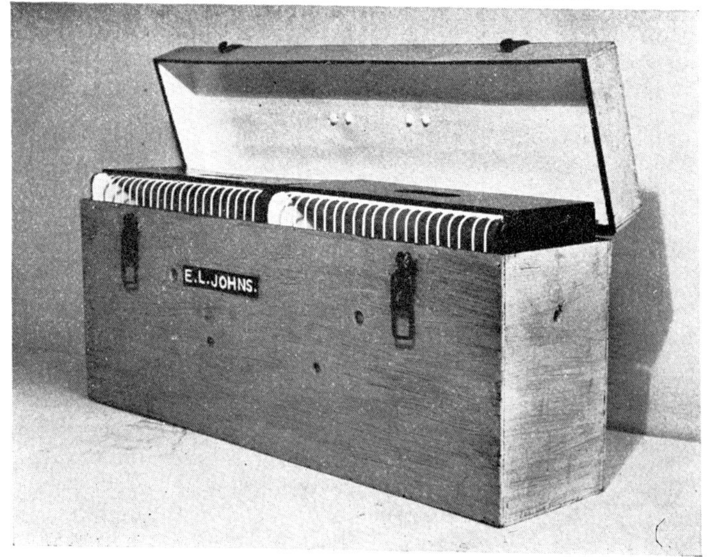

From my own experience with our pet Georgie, who is now a year old, I do not feel that it is difficult to teach a budgie to talk. But there is much more chance of a budgie talking if it is obtained at an early age, as at this age it is usually fairly tame and soon settles down. After that it is up to you, patience being a great virtue. Our own pet, for instance, was very quiet the first week. Then he began to 'chatter' in the normal budgie fashion. We kept repeating his name, Georgie, to him. After a week of teaching him this word all my family claimed he was saying it. If he was it was in very poor English, but, as I have already said, by the time he was about twelve weeks old he could repeat his name clearly and is now constantly quoting new phrases. He has about twenty sayings, but this is a small repertoire compared to many. With any talking budgie the 'sky's the limit'. It is up to those who train it.

At one of the annual national exhibitions of cage birds, in London, one budgie on exhibition was known to have a vocabulary of over 300 words. There is no reason why your pet should not be equally talented with patience and teaching.

FIVE

Breeding

Many who buy a single budgie as a pet often become so enthralled by it that they feel they would like to keep more and breed them—in fact this is how I started.

I had always been passionately fond of birds and had kept canaries, finch mules (these were bred from one parent who was a canary and the other a British finch, the male birds were wonderful songsters) and several varieties of pigeons, and poultry; but it was when I married that I first became acquainted with budgies. One day I noticed in the local paper that there were young ones for sale. This was very unusual as they were very scarce just after the war. I immediately went to the place advertised and managed to obtain one. So started my 'budgie fever', a complaint I have suffered with ever since. But once you have kept a few budgies they become part of your life, and to be without them is to feel lost. So, as some of you are perhaps contemplating breeding them, I thought it would be worthwhile to give some details about this.

The first necessity is, of course, a cage. A box cage is the best for breeding. A suitable size for one pair of budgies to breed in would be 2 feet 6 inches long, 18 inches high and 18 inches wide, but a larger cage would be even better.

A larger cage that I have found useful is one 5 feet in length, with the same height and width as the single breeding cage just mentioned. This could be made so that a removable partition could be fitted into the middle, and when the partition is in place you have two breeding compartments. When this is taken out you have a handy length cage in which to keep several budgies when they are not breeding. This type is known as a flight-cage.

When you make cages it is advisable to fit trays in the bottom of them. If this is done they can be removed and the cleaning is then very much easier, whereas if you do not have these trays cleaning is more difficult, and the original bottom of the cage becomes soiled and worn.

Assuming that you now have the cages and have obtained the necessary food that I mentioned in a previous chapter, we will now consider the number of birds you will require.

Budgies are gregarious. By that we mean that they like to have other budgies around them particularly when breeding, and so for those of you who want to breed these little birds, it is advisable to have two or more pairs. I know of some instances where a person has kept only one pair of budgies and has been very successful in breeding with them, but also know of many others, including myself, who have tried breeding with one pair only and had no success whatsoever. So to increase your chance of success please start with two or three pairs.

There are other reasons why it is advisable to have more than one pair when breeding. For instance, if you have one pair only and something happens to one of them during breeding, this often means the loss of the eggs and any youngsters which are in the nest; but if you happen to have other pairs breeding at the same time you can transfer the eggs and youngsters to other nests, and frequently save some of the young birds.

In the normal course of events the average budgie hen is a wonderfully devoted mother, and so what I have said about transferring eggs and perhaps youngsters to other nests, is only done as a last resort, and not as routine, and my remarks about something happening to them during breeding should not be taken to mean that budgies often die when breeding. This is not so. But where livestock is concerned things like this do happen occasionally, and so if we have several pairs of budgies, and anything like this occurs we can not only cope with the situation more easily, but we do not feel the disappointment as bitterly as if we had only one pair.

Having said this, we now come to the details that we need to know before purchasing stock.

When buying budgies for breeding, it is an advantage to select hen birds that have never been used for breeding before, as budgies, like all living things, are creatures of habit. If you buy hen birds that have been brought up in different surroundings and have become accustomed to breeding in a type of nest-box unlike your own, you will often find that you have difficulty in getting them to breed, so when purchasing your initial stock it is advisable to buy young hens. That way you will have birds that will be used to breeding in your type of cage etc.

Perhaps you want to know the youngest age at which a hen budgie will breed? A good age to start a hen breeding is about eleven months' old, although they will breed at a very much earlier age. Cock birds can be mated for breeding at ten months. Hen birds will usually breed well for three seasons before they become less reliable, although there are exceptions. I myself had a hen which was a good breeder when she was six years old, but this is very unusual. Cock birds will often still be good breeders at this age. So you see, by buying young birds and keeping them for breeding, with good fortune you could have the service of these birds for several years.

When pairing-up the birds for breeding, if you have bought some older birds, pair these with younger ones. For instance, if you have a three-year-old cock bird it would make an ideal mate for an eleven-month-old hen. Fanciers very rarely pair two young or two old birds together, when breeding it is usually best to pair an old bird with a young one.

Many people who take up the hobby of budgies with the aim of breeding them, become disappointed and disheartened because they do not do very well when they first start. Of course, there is no fast rule to success, but I think that one of the primary reasons for this is that often the person concerned does not give the newly-bought birds time to settle down. I said previously that budgies are creatures of habit. When you buy your birds, you must realize that they need time to get used to their cage, to you, and to the environment in which they are kept. If you have the foresight and patience to buy the birds you require several months before you intend to start breeding you have a greater chance of success in breeding them.

Now assuming that you have bought the birds you need with which to start breeding, you should now keep the cock birds from the hens, as the saying "absence makes the heart grow fonder" is as true with regard to budgies as it is with people. Not only does keeping them apart make them keener to breed, but also helps to keep them fit. Often if you keep the sexes together, you will find that the cock birds will feed the hens continuously, the result being that the cock birds will be very thin, and the hens far too fat, which is a bad fault in breeding stock.

We will now imagine that your stock is breeding fit, and waiting to be paired for breeding. You notice that the hens are biting at bits of wood in the cage, and that the cocks are restless and calling the hens, so now you catch the pairs and put them in the cages you are going to use for breeding. You notice that one pair are very friendly immediately, and the cock bird is beginning to feed the hen, whilst another pair are not very friendly, in fact they are almost fighting. Sometimes they will never agree, and will continue to fight each other, but often the pair which seemed to hate each other at the beginning will become very friendly and are the most successful pair when breeding.

We should leave the pairs together for a couple of days before we fix the nest-box for them to use. Many fanciers fix the nest-box before the pair are put in the cage, but from my own experience I do not think this is always wise, as some hen budgies are so keen to go to nest that they forget their mate, and lay eggs before they have mated, the result being that often there are several eggs but no chicks. Pairing up the birds for a few days before giving them a nest-box will usually obviate this, and also allow the birds time to get used to one another before the hen becomes seriously interested in the nest-box.

As the nest-box is a very important item in breeding, it is appropriate that I should give you some particulars of this equipment.

We should remember that the wild budgies nest in holes in trees. They usually nest in the trunk of a tree which is partly rotten, and they bite away at the rotten part until they have sufficient room for their nest-hole.

They do not use anything to line the nest. When budgies were first kept in enclosures, several sorts of nesting receptacles were used, logs with holes cut out, and shells of the coconut were examples, but these were found to be anything but hygienic. The present-day nest-box was found to be the best, as it could be cleaned out easily. This box is very simple and it can be square, oblong or upright.

To help those of you who are not very keen on making things, I would mention that nest-boxes can be purchased from pet stores for a moderate price; but, whether you buy them or make them yourselves, the basic point of the nest-boxes should be that they are big enough to hold the pair of birds breeding and any youngsters that they produce. Therefore, providing this is so, it makes very little difference what type is used.

All nest-boxes should have a block of wood approximately one inch thick (this thickness helps to keep the eggs at an even temperature), fitted into the bottom. This should be chiselled out, so that the circle resembles the shape of a saucer. This is known as a nest concave, and assists in keeping the eggs in the centre when the hen is sitting on them.

The nest-box should also have a round hole about 1¾ inches in diameter, and a small perch beneath, fitted so that the birds can get in and out easily.

The eggs are plain white and are laid every other day. If fertile they will hatch eighteen days after incubation, but it does not always follow that the first egg, even if fertile, will always hatch eighteen days after being laid, as often the hen bird will lay two or three eggs before she begins to sit on them in earnest. In this case they will be a few days late in hatching and you may get two chicks hatching at roughly the same time.

The number of eggs laid varies considerably. Some lay only one or two, and I have had hens which have laid as many as eleven. There is no fast rule as to how many eggs will be laid, but a rough average would be about five. After about seven days, if the eggs are fertile, they will have a more solid look and a definite whiter appearance.

Presuming the eggs hatch you will find that the youngsters look very tiny at first, but they are wiry little things, and provided their parents feed and look after them properly, they will grow very quickly.

A few days after being born a fluffy down will appear on them, (for those of you who intend to breed and exhibit budgies, it is essential that the youngsters have a special closed budgie ring put on them between six to nine days old. These rings are completely closed and can only be put on when the chick's leg is small, I will mention further about ringing and give details, in another part of the book.) About the third week you will begin to notice the proper feathers coming on the chick, and by about six weeks it will have its complete plumage. At this age, once you are certain it can feed itself, you can remove it from its parents, but please be sure it can eat properly, as many young birds die due to being taken from their parents at too early an age, so don't be too keen to remove them, as in the life of a young bird a couple of days can make a world of difference. To assist the youngsters just taken from their parents, when you put them in another cage, see that a small dish of water is placed on the bottom of the cage, and also that seed, besides being available in a dish, is also scattered over the floor. In a few days they will be eating from the dishes, but until they get used to these, they will pick up seed from the bottom of the cage. This is only a small matter, but it is extremely important, as some young birds at first seem very dull at finding the seed, and must be helped to do this.

As I have stated previously, a budgie gets its first plumage (complete feathers) about six weeks after it is born, and up to the time that it has its first moult it is known as a 'barhead'. This is due to the fact that most varieties of normal and opaline budgies have, until about three months of age, 'barring' or 'grizzling' across the head. When a youngster begins to moult he or she loses this 'barring'. When it has completed its first adult moult at approximately five months, the colour across its head becomes clear.

Lutinos (red-eyed clear yellows), albinos (red-eyed clear whites) or black-eyed clear youngsters do not show the 'barhead' characteristic when in nest-feather plumage but can be identified as youngsters, as their colour is 'washy' and lacks lustre. Once they have moulted, their colour becomes much brighter and more attractive to look at.

SIX

The History of the Budgie

It is a remarkable fact that although the budgie is kept by millions of people as a pet, comparatively few of them know anything of its history or where it came from originally. In this chapter, I am briefly going to mention these points so that you may know a little more about your charming pet.

The original wild budgie came to this country from Australia in 1840. John Gould, the famous explorer and naturalist, returned to England and amongst several live birds he brought back with him were a pair of small green parakeets, which we all know now as budgies. This was the first wild pair ever imported into Great Britain, and I doubt if John Gould ever visualized how popular the budgerigar was to become throughout the world—although it was over ninety years before it really became so well loved as a pet.

But let us go back to how John Gould first saw the budgerigar in its wild state. It should be remembered that the budgie is gregarious by nature. Since they are grass parakeets with seeding grass as their basic diet, it was quite common to see budgies flying together, often in numbers of many thousands, looking for the rich seeding grasses on which they thrived. John Gould often had the wonderful experience of seeing thousands of budgies in various stages eating, drinking, sleeping and at times flying together.

When the breeding season was in progress, they lived even closer together than before, and it was not uncommon for five or six nesting holes to be situated in the trunk of one tree.

The famous explorer observed that all the budgies were the same colour—green, the colour of grass. In the budgerigar fancy these are known as 'light greens'.

John Gould was fascinated by them and brought a pair to England in 1840. They were watched with interest, as it was wondered if they would live in such a climate as England. Surprisingly, in a few weeks, they had completely settled down, and treated the variation of the English climate with indifference.

Most of those who saw them for the first time were captivated by them, and as time went by more budgerigars were brought into Britain and imported into other European countries, and eventually these bred in captivity. Then the remarkable happened; they produced colour mutations, that is other colours than the original light green. The first new colour was the yellow, which appeared for the first time in 1872; and in the early 1880s the sky-blue was bred. As the years passed other colour mutations appeared.

And so we come to 1925. By this time there were, scattered over Britain, quite a few fanciers who kept and bred budgies. They felt there was a great future for the bird, and so a meeting was convened. Twelve fanciers attended and founded the Budgerigar Club with the aim of promoting interest in this bird and establishing the budgerigar as an exhibition variety.

From the start the Budgerigar Club made steady progress, with many fanciers joining and taking up the breeding of budgies. Later the Budgerigar Club became known as the Budgerigar Society, which today has a membership of many thousands.

With many people breeding budgerigars, they became more numerous, and further colour mutations turned up, so that by the late 1920s they were being exhibited in pairs at many of the shows. Pairs were also kept as pets.

Then around 1930 a discovery was made that was eventually to make the budgie the most loved pet bird in the world.

This simple discovery was that if a young budgie was kept on its own as soon as it was old enough to look after itself, it would not only make a wonderful pet, but, even more remarkable, if trained would talk. This was a revelation, as previously the belief was that budgies, being gregarious, would not live on their own, and were always kept in pairs or groups. When it became known that they would live if kept singly and also talk, they immediately became famous and were the most sought-after birds in the world. Around the early 1930s instances were quoted of foreign princes paying as much as £250 for a budgie to give to their loved ones.

And so from the time of the discovery that budgies could talk, the popularity of these lovable creatures as pets has constantly increased.

Many thousands of fanciers breed them for exhibiting, and often at shows more than 1,000 budgies will be on view. Yes, the future for the budgie looks very, very bright, as this remarkable little bird has the wonderful gift of captivating everyone with whom it comes in contact and is quite capable of changing the life of anybody who keeps one.

SEVEN

Colours in Budgies, and how to Breed them

In this chapter I will begin by describing most of the colours of budgies which can be obtained. Then I will give you some brief details about colour factors in these birds, and about matings—which I hope will help you to see how particular colours can be bred.

The genetics I am going to mention are very elementary, as my aim right through this book has been to make it as easy as possible for the reader to understand the subject I am discussing. I have therefore only delved briefly into colour inheritance, which can bewilder the newcomer to the fancy if described in too complex a manner. For those of you who wish to go deeper into colour genetics, and budgerigar matters in general, I mention some excellent books on the subject at the back of this book.

From the original light-green budgies there have now been bred over 100 colours or combination of colours. Some of these, if put side by side, would look similar, but if inspected closely would be found to vary in some way.

The basic shades of green are light-green, dark-green, olive-green and grey-green. When these have what is known as 'normal' markings—which are the same as the original wild budgies—the wings are black and yellow.

The basic colours of the blue series are sky-blue, cobalt, violet, mauve and grey. When these are normals, their wing markings are black and white. Usually these have white faces, but they can be bred with yellow faces and so are described as yellow-face blues or greys. All these various shades of greens, blues or grey can be bred with different coloured wings, such as clear wings, grey-wings and cinnamon-wings.

There are also pieds, fallows and various yellows and whites, plus the greatly admired clear-coloured budgies, such as lutinos, which are pure yellow with red eyes; albinos, which are pure white with red eyes; and two of the newer colours, the black-eyed clear yellow, and the black-eyed clear white.

There is also the opaline factor, which gives the bird a different pattern of markings to the 'normal'. So an opaline, although having the same body colour as a normal, would have different markings on its head and between its wings (which is known as its mantle), and would also differ on the wings. The wing colour would also be changed—as, for instance, in a normal sky-blue it would be black and white, whereas in an opaline sky-blue the markings would be black and sky-blue in colour. The opaline factor can be bred in all colours except lutinos, albinos and black-eyed clears.

There are some really beautiful budgerigars which have several colours in their make-up, one such coloured variety is the 'rainbow'. This bird has most of the colours of the rainbow in its plumage, and, like the rainbow, it is in pastel shades. As you look at this budgie in the sunlight you can see many hues of the rainbow shining through its feathers. Yes, the name of rainbow for this coloured budgie is very apt!

Whilst quoting the various colours of budgerigars, I

would like to mention four colours which invariably confuse the newcomer to the budgerigar fancy. Two of them are the olive-green and the grey-green, which are very much alike, but here Nature has come to our assistance and given them different coloured tails and cheek patches: in the olive-green the tail is navy blue and the cheek patches royal blue, whilst the grey-green has a black tail and grey cheek patches. The other two colours which are so alike are the mauve and the grey. Here the mauve has a navy-blue tail and royal-blue cheek patches, and the grey, which is closely related to the grey-green, has a black tail and grey cheek patches.

You can see from the brief description of some of the colours, how really wonderful it is that all these colours should have evolved over the years from the original light green. In fact, budgies have been bred in every body colour except red and black. Some say these will never appear but who can be sure? The other colours appeared purely by chance (mutation) and not through any effort of man, and who is to say that the red, or the black budgie will not turn up in the same way? Only time will tell.

We will now go on to genetics and colour inheritance in these birds.

Although it is not simple to understand colour genetics in budgerigars, breeders who learn the basic principles of colour heredity can pair (mate) their birds with almost certain knowledge of the colour of the resultant offspring.

To give us an elementary knowledge of colour inheritance, we must remember first that green is dominant to blue, so if you mate a pure light-green to a sky-blue you will get all light-green youngsters. These youngsters, through having one parent which was blue, are known as green-split-blue. (When describing the word 'split' in writing we use an oblique stroke, thus a green-split-blue would be described as green/blue.) If two of these green/blue budgies were paired, the fact that they were both carrying the blue factor (which green-split-blue means) would result in a percentage of both green and blue offspring.

Another mating, a green/blue paired to a blue coloured mate will produce on average an even larger percentage of blue youngsters, but there will be some green/blue as well.

But although two green-coloured budgies which are split blue will produce some blue chicks as well as greens when mated, it is impossible to breed green offspring from a pair of blue-coloured budgies.

Often greys, when mated together, will produce some blue young amongst their progeny, but it is not possible to obtain grey offspring from a pair of blues.

Next we should bear in mind that in budgies there are three basic groups of colours (shades), these are light, medium and dark, and each budgie (other than lutinos, albinos and black-eyed clears) is in one of these groups which we call factors. Light-greens or sky-blues for instance are light or single-factor coloured birds. These light-greens or sky-blues could be normal, opaline, clear-wings, cinnamon, greywings etc., yet the fact that their body colour is either light-green or sky-blue means that they are light factor and will breed as such.

Dark-greens, cobalts and visual violets (these are cobalts with the violet colour factor in them) are medium factor species, having one light and one dark factor.

The dark factor colours are the mauve and the olive-green. Both these colours have two dark factors, and whatever these birds are mated with they will never produce light or single-factor colours. Two dark-factor birds paired together will produce all dark-factor chicks.

(Left) The Budgerigar Society's ideal budgerigar (reproduced by courtesy of the Budgerigar Society). *(Right)* An exhibition light-green normal cock

(Left) Three different varieties of budgies. Left to right: the newest mutation, the dominant pied; the normal, whose markings resemble the original wild species; the opaline. *(Right)* The albino, which has red eyes and a clear white body

And a dark factor mated to a light factor gives us all medium-factor offspring. Whereas a dark-factor bird mated to a medium factor will produce 50 per cent of both medium and dark-factor young.

MATING TABLE

Here are some pair matings, with their colour expectations to help you further to understand how the colours are bred.

Pure light-green x pure light-green.	Produces all light-green progeny, both being light-factor colours.
Light-green/blue x light-green/blue.	Gives you 75 per cent light-green offspring. Some of these will be pure light-green, and some will be light-green/blue, and will have to be test mated to see which are split blue. The other 25 per cent will be sky-blue in colour from this mating.
Sky-blue (light-factor) x mauve (dark-factor).	Produces all cobalt, which is a medium-factor colour.
Cobalt x cobalt.	Throws young of all three blue colour groups, because cobalts, being medium factor birds, do not breed true like the light and dark factor colours. The expectation from mating cobalts together are 50 per cent cobalts, 25 per cent sky-blues and 25 per cent mauves.
Cobalt x mauve.	Gives 50 per cent of each of these colours.
Sky-blue x cobalt.	Breeds 50 per cent of each.
Sky-blue x olive/blue.	Produces 50 per cent cobalts, 50 per cent dark-green type 1.
Light-green/blue x mauve.	Expectancy: 50 per cent cobalts, 50 per cent dark-green type 2.
Pure light-green x pure olive-green.	Is a mating where we get all medium-factor birds, these being dark-greens.

Having given you some mating tables and their expectations I am now going to mention another group of colours, the sex-linked varieties. If these are understood in conjunction with what I have already stated about the light, medium and dark-factor colour groups, it will help you considerably towards having a good basic understanding of colour inheritance in budgerigar breeding.

There are four groups of budgies whose breeding is sex-linked. One group is the opaline. A further sex-linked colour is the cinnamon, whose wing markings are a cinnamon-chocolate colour and whose body colour is paler than in the orthodox normal and opaline green and blue series of budgies. The other two sex-linked colours are the lutino and the albino.

When it comes to producing these sex-linked varieties, although they are totally different in appearance, they all follow a similar pattern of sex-linked heredity in their breeding sequence.

By sex-linkage we mean that often it is the owner who decides whether he or she breed will breed certain sex-linked coloured varieties, purely by mating a certain coloured cock bird with a particular coloured hen. So sex-linked is simply the mating of certain colours of a certain sex to determine whether sex-linked budgies will be bred, and also whether they will be cocks or hens or both. As all sex-linked varieties breed to the same rule of genetics, for simplicity I am going to quote a mating table for one of these, the opaline; but should you become interested in one of the other sex-linked varieties (cinnamons, lutinos, albinos) and you substitute one of these colours in place of the opaline, you will find the expectations of the sex-linkage the same.

Here are some of the matings, showing the sex-linkage expectations:

Opaline x opaline.	Give all opaline progeny.
Opaline cock x ordinary hen.	Produce all hens with the opaline characteristic, and cocks of ordinary colours which are split opaline.
Ordinary split opaline cock x opaline hen.	Gives half the offspring both cocks and hens showing the opaline character. The other half being 25 per cent of ordinary hens, and ordinary split opaline cocks.
Pure ordinary cock x opaline hen.	This is an interesting mating as, although the hen is sex-linked, no progeny are bred from this pairing which are visually sex-linked. The expectations are all ordinary hens, and all ordinary split opaline cocks.
Ordinary split opaline cock x ordinary hen.	Produce opaline and ordinary hens, ordinary split opaline cocks, and pure ordinary cocks, as these cocks are visually alike they must be test-mated to ascertain whether they are pure ordinary cocks, or split opaline.

Note Ordinary refers to coloured varieties of budgies which are not sex-linked.

Finally, on the subject of sex-linkage, we should remember that an ordinary hen cannot be split for a sex-linked colour, even if one of its parents was.

As I stated at the beginning of this chapter, I have only mentioned a few details of colour genetics in budgerigars. And perhaps to you who are reading this it seems terribly complicated. This is not really so. Once you have a few budgies and know what the colours are that you have been reading about, it becomes much more simple to understand, and to the newcomer to the budgerigar fancy who really wants to know all about these wonderful birds, and how their various colours can be reproduced, colour genetics is fascinating!

EIGHT

Your Questions Answered

During the number of years that I have kept budgerigars, I have found that once someone knows this there are numerous questions he wants to ask me. As I have been asked some of the questions perhaps hundreds of times I am going to quote them in this chapter, and hope you will find them both interesting and helpful.

To commence, here is a question that I have been asked probably most of all! How long does a budgie usually live?

I would say on average five to six years, but it varies greatly. I knew of one which lived until it was fourteen, and I personally have had them live to ten years old; but about five to six years is a good life span for a budgie.

However, I think many more pets would live to a much older age, if they were allowed to be more active. I say this as many owners kill their birds with kindness. They want their bird to be happy so, thinking they are being kind, they put too many toys, ladders and gadgets in the cage. The result is that the poor bird can hardly move, let alone enjoy itself, and eventually gives up trying to, becomes fat and unhealthy and dies much earlier than it need have done, purely because of its owner's misguided kindness. So please, in your pet's interest, see that it has ample room in its cage to move freely and flap its wings if it wants to, as natural movement is the finest tonic of all. When you can spare the time let your bird out for a fly around (of course, making sure before you do this that all the doors and windows are shut). By doing this your pet will not only be healthier but will live longer.

Another question often asked is should I give my bird household food to eat?

Definitely not, bits of pastry and other scraps are too rich for budgies and can cause ill health. It is much better to keep to a plain diet and the extras that I have mentioned in a previous chapter.

At what age are baby budgies old enough to leave their mother? Just over six weeks is the earliest that youngsters should be taken from their parents, and then only if it is certain that they can eat seed. I am sorry to say that often breeders are not sure of this when they sell them, with the result that sometimes they die a day or so after being purchased. I speak from experience, as the first budgie I ever owned died a day after I bought it purely because the breeder was not certain if it would feed itself, and took a chance instead of asking me to wait a day or so. The result was that the bird died of starvation. So please if any of you reading this eventually breed some budgies of your own, always be sure that the young birds can eat before taking them from their parents.

How can I get my pet budgie to bathe; he won't go near a bath? It is true that many budgies are very reluctant to bathe, and some will not do so under any circumstances, but sometimes a budgie can be induced to bathe by placing a leaf of lettuce or cabbage in the bottom of the bath. This somehow seems to take away their fear of water and so they will bathe. Strangely, budgies in open wire aviaries will often bathe, not by going into a bath or dish, but by rubbing themselves in the wet grass and getting themselves thoroughly wet. They will also do this when the aviary is covered with snow and seem indifferent to the cold, and yet the birds very rarely bathe in water. This seems to be one of the peculiarities of the budgie.

Frequently I meet people at bird shows and they ask what a judge looks for when he is judging budgies.

Although to anyone visiting a show for the first time it might appear that all the budgerigars look the same, this is not really so, as all the various colours have their own characteristics, virtues and faults, and so they are judged accordingly, each colour having a scale of points. Should there be a perfect bird (there has not been one bred yet!), it would receive 100 points, but just to give an example of how the points are awarded I am going to quote the scale of points for the normal light green, which is as follows, this of course being for the perfect specimen:

Size, shape, balance and deportment	45
Size and shape of head	20
Colour	15
Mask and spots	15
Wing markings	5
	100

So you see that the ideal budgie on the show bench must be good all over to win the premier awards.

Next, many people, having once been to a show, where they have noticed that most of the budgies have closed metal rings on their legs, want to know the following: if I want to exhibit budgies must they be wearing a ring?

No, it is not necessary for budgies to be ringed for

exhibition, but if they are not close ringed they must be shown in the any-age or adult classes, irrespective of the age of the bird. (Close ringed means that the ring is put on the bird when only a few days old. When the bird's leg grows it cannot be taken off, and so remains on the bird for the duration of its life.) If the bird is ringed with the official ring issued through the Budgerigar Society (to obtain these you must be a member of the Budgerigar Society or an area society affiliated to it) for the current year, that is the year they are born, they can be exhibited that year and until the 28th February of the following year in what is known as breeder's classes.

These classes are for budgies which have been bred and exhibited by the breeder, and it is these classes that give the breeder a thrill to win, as it is always an honour to win with birds you have bred yourself. So, by ringing budgies with your own Budgerigar Society official code number and year on them, you prove that they were actually bred by you.

So you see that, although you can exhibit budgies whether they are ringed or not, if you intend to do this seriously and achieve success, it means breeding your own. Therefore much is to be gained through ringing your birds with the official rings of the Budgerigar Society and showing them in the appropriate classes, but you should note that only those bred and ringed with the official ring (not closed metal ones that can be bought at pet stores and are not recognized by show societies) can compete during the current year in the breeder's classes.

Another query frequently asked by the potential breeder is: I am thinking about ringing my birds, can you advise me about this?

Firstly, if you are definitely going to ring your birds, you should join the Budgerigar Society or affiliated area

RINGING

(*above left*) Hold chick in left hand. With the first finger and thumb of this hand bring the three long toes together and told them in position by the ball of the foot. Hold the ring in the right hand and with the first finger and thumb slide it over the three long toes.

(*above right*) The ring is placed over the ball of the foot.

(*above left*) Gently grasp the three long toes with the first finger and thumb of the right hand, and at the same time take the ring between the first finger and thumb of the left hand. Carefully slide the ring up the leg as near to the hock as possible. At this stage the short back toe is held by the ring against the leg and is partly hidden (usually only the claw of the back toe being visible). Insert the burnt matchstick between the toe and leg and gently prize the back toe through the ring, so that this toe is now through the ring with the three long toes, and the ring is fully on.

(*above right*) Showing the position of the ring when ringing is completed.

society or both. By doing this you can obtain the official closed rings with your own code number on them so that any birds wearing these rings will be officially registered as having been bred by you.

The rings should be placed on the youngster around six to seven days old. Sometimes the ring will slip off. If this should happen it denotes that the leg is too small to hold the ring, and it should be put on again the next day, when the leg will be just that shade bigger. But never leave it too late, it is better to ring the bird too soon—even if the ring falls off and has to be replaced—than to leave it until the chick is ten days old or so, and too big for the ring to be put on its leg.

Most fanciers have had the experience of leaving it too late to ring a youngster, then having the disappointment of seeing the youngster turn out to be a 'beauty' and not being able to show it in the breeders classes because it was not ringed.

When the birds are near the time for ringing, if it is at all possible get an experienced fancier to show you how to put the rings on. If there is not a fancier available in your area, and you decide to ring them yourselves, do not be in too great a hurry to get it over. Naturally you will be a bit concerned the first time you ring a bird but if you take your time and do it methodically you will do it successfully and in a matter of seconds.

You will need a matchstick as an implement when you are ringing a bird. Strike the match, let it burn for a moment, then blow it out and rub off the charcoal, so that it is not too pointed, which might hurt the chick being ringed.

Having got the matchstick and the ring available, take the chick from the nest, and if you are right-handed hold it in the left hand. Let the chick lay on its back. With the first finger and thumb of the left hand gather the three toes together and hold them in position by the ball of the foot. Pick up the ring with the right hand and, using the thumb and first finger, slide it over the three longest toes—this will bring these three toes partly through the ring. Gently grasp these toes with the first finger and thumb of the right hand and at the same time take the ring between the first finger and thumb of the left hand, gradually slide the ring up the leg as near to the hock as possible, the short toe being held by the ring against the leg. Insert the burnt matchstick between the toe and leg and gently prise it through the ring, so that all the toes are through, and the ring is fitting nicely on the shank of the leg.

This sounds an awfully complicated operation, but it isn't. However, never ring a bird if you are in a hurry. It must be done patiently. Have everything prepared including several spare matchsticks (it is surprising how they seem to vanish when you require them). If this is done everything will be satisfactory.

Now to another query owners often ask. Why is it my pet budgie is always losing some of its feathers?

It is quite natural for budgies to have a complete moult annually. This takes place in the autumn, any time from September to November and last about six weeks. Some also have what we call a 'partial' moult. This happens in the early spring, when over a period of two or three weeks they cast some of their feathers.

But when a bird constantly loses its feathers, it is a sign that something is wrong. This condition is known as soft-moult, and, although it might make a budgie feel a little 'off-colour', it is not so much the state of its health which causes this condition, but the environment in which it is living.

For a bird to have good health and nice feather

condition, it is essential that it lives in an even temperature. A kitchen (where many pets seem to be kept) is not suitable, unless there is nowhere else to keep it. As an example of what a bird endures when placed in a kitchen, I will give the conditions it has to tolerate. In the mornings, with all the cooking in full swing, the heat is so intense that it can hardly breathe. Then after lunch the room becomes much cooler, and by the middle of the afternoon it is quite cold for the bird. Tea-time arrives and the place becomes once again hot and unpleasant for our pet, but in all probability it will suffer most of all during the night, as this is the coldest time of all. So it has to endure excessive heat by day and cold conditions by night. Naturally its body becomes upset, and protests by constantly shedding its feathers.

Nothing upsets birds (whether budgies, canaries, foreign or British birds) more than constant fluctuations in temperature. Therefore if it is possible keep your bird in a room other than the kitchen; also avoid placing it near a draughty position, such as by the door. It is also advisable never to keep a bird in the bay of a window, as it is not only draughty, but, like the kitchen, very rarely a comfortable temperature for a bird. If there is no heat at night in the room where your pet sleeps, cover the top half of the cage with a thin cloth. This will help to prevent your bird feeling the draught.

You can also assist to counteract soft-moult by placing a bath or dish of water in the cage on fine days. The best time to do this is in the morning so that the bird can thoroughly dry out its feathers before going to roost for the night. There is nothing finer to stimulate health than bathing, and once your pet is in good health it will not only stop casting its feathers constantly, but will be better in every way!

When I meet people at bird shows they invariably ask whether you get a lot of money if your birds win first prizes?

In fact no. The actual prize money is very small. Some of the shows may pay £1, but most pay half of this or less. So you can see that when you have to buy special cages, (which are all identical and are made to the Budgerigar Society's pattern) to show your budgies in, and to pay the entrance fee etc., the idea of winning a fortune at a show is pure myth. It is the honour that is gained, not the money. But competition is so keen that often exhibitors will pay fairly high prices to obtain quality exhibition budgies to improve their stock, and it is through these sales that outstandingly successful exhibitors make money, as often they keep several hundred budgies and sell perhaps half each year. When numbers like this are sold by one breeder, it can be appreciated that there is a large cash turn-over, but a fancier such as this has considerable expenses for feeding so much stock, as well as the upkeep of the equipment etc. Add to this the large sums breeders have to pay to obtain even better birds than they already have to keep their studs outstanding, and you can see that even these very successful fanciers do not make enormous sums.

Many fanciers who keep a small number of birds for exhibition, usually sell their surplus show stock in the price range between £3 and £10 each, but most of these fanciers, after deducting their expenses for the upkeep of their stock, usually purchase better-quality exhibition birds with the remainder, so you see it is only the minority of fanciers who keep budgies for exhibition who ever make any real profit worth mentioning.

But there are many who keep budgies purely for breeding pets. These fanciers are not interested in pedigree birds or their colours, but only in breeding large numbers of them, which in most cases they sell at reasonable prices, I imagine these fanciers make more money from their birds than the average back-yard budgerigar exhibitor, whose sole aim is to produce better-quality show birds for his or her own satisfaction, with profit being of secondary importance.

Having mentioned exhibition budgerigars in this chapter from time to time, I thought it would be appropriate to include the Budgerigar Society's standard for the ideal budgerigar, and also this society's scale of points for each individual standardized coloured variety. These are produced by the very kind permission of the Budgerigar Society.

As you will see the standard for the ideal budgerigar gives complete detail of what the perfect exhibition budgerigar should be, whilst the scale of points for the various colours is an excellent guide both to those whose aim is to breed the ideal exhibition budgie of a certain colour, and to those who have to judge them.

THE BUDGERIGAR SOCIETY'S STANDARD FOR THE IDEAL BUDGERIGAR

CONDITION is essential. If a bird is not in condition it should never be considered for any award.

TYPE—Gracefully tapered from nape of neck to tip of tail, with an approximately straight back line, and a rather deep nicely curved chest.

LENGTH—The ideal length is eight-and-a-half inches from the crown of the head to the tip of the tail. Wings well braced, carried just above the cushion of the tail and not crossed. The ideal length of the wing is three-and-three-quarter inches from the butt to the tip of the longest primary flight, which must contain seven visual primary flight feathers fully grown and not broken. NO BIRD SHOWING 'LONG-FLIGHTED' CHARACTERISTICS SHALL BE ELIGIBLE TO TAKE ANY AWARD.

HEAD—Large, round, wide and symetrical when viewed from any angle; curvature of skull commencing at cere, to lift outward and upward, continuing over the top and to base of head in one graceful sweep.

BEAK—Set well into face.

EYE—to be bold and bright, and positioned well away from front, top and back skull.

NECK—to be short and wide when viewed from either side or front.

WINGS—Approximately two-fifths the total length of the bird, well braced, carried just above the cushion of the tail and not crossed.

TAIL to be straight and tight with two long tail feathers.

POSITION—Steady on perch at an angle of 30 degrees from the vertical, looking fearless and natural.

MASK AND SPOTS—Mask to be clear, deep and wide, ornamented by six evenly spaced large round throat spots, the outer two being partially covered at the base by cheek patches, the size of the spots to be in proportion to the rest of the make-up of the bird as shown in the Ideals published by The Budgerigar Society. Spots can be either too large or too small.

LEGS AND FEET—Legs should be straight and strong, with two front and two rear toes and claws firmly gripping perch.

MARKINGS—Wavy markings on cheek, head, neck, back and wings to stand out clearly.

COLOUR—Clear and level and of an even shade.

THE BUDGERIGAR SOCIETY'S SCALE OF POINTS

Remember:

Condition is supremely important.

TYPE	Size, shape, balance and deportment	Size and shape of head	Colour	Mask and spots	Wing markings
Green (Light, Dark or Olive)	45	20	15	15	5
Grey Green (Light, Medium or Dark)	45	20	15	15	5
Yellow (incldg. Op. Yel. but excldg. Lutino)	45	20	35	—	—
Olive Yellow (incldg. Cinnamon Olive Yellow)	45	20	35	—	—
Skyblue, Cobalt, Mauve or Violet ...	45	20	15	15	5
Grey (Light, Medium or Dark) ...	45	20	15	15	5
White (light suffusion—including Opaline White but excluding Albino)	45	20	*35	—	—
Whitewing (Skyblue, Cobalt, Mauve, Violet or Grey)	45	20	*35	—	—
Yellow-wing (Light, Dark, Olive or Grey Green)	45	20	*35	—	—
Greywing (Light, Dark, Olive or Grey Green)	45	20	10	10	15
Greywing (Skyblue, Cobalt, Mauve, Violet or Grey)	45	20	10	10	15
Cinnamon (Light, Dark, Olive or Grey Green)	45	20	10	10	15
Cinnamon (Skyblue, Cobalt, Mauve, Violet or Grey)	45	20	10	10	15
Fallow (Light, Dark, Olive or Grey Green)	45	20	15	15	5
Fallow (Skyblue, Cobalt, Mauve, Violet or Grey)	45	20	15	15	5
Lutino	45	20	35	—	—
Albino	45	20	35	—	—
Opaline (Light, Dark, Olive or Grey Green)	40	20	†25	10	5
Opaline (Skyblue, Cobalt, Mauve, Violet or Grey)	40	20	†25	10	5
Opaline Cinnamon (Light, Dark, Olive or Grey Green)	40	20	†25	10	5
Opaline Cinnamon (Skyblue, Cobalt, Mauve, Violet or Grey)	40	20	†25	10	5
Opaline Greywing (Light, Dark, Olive or Grey Green)	40	20	†25	10	5

Remember:

Condition is supremely important.

TYPE	Size, shape, balance and deportment	Size and shape of head	Colour	Mask and spots	Wing markings
Opaline Greywing (Skyblue, Cobalt, Mauve, Violet or Grey)	40	20	†25	10	5
Yellow-faced (all varieties in Blue series except Pieds)	45	20	15	15	5
Pied (Dominant varieties)	45	20	§15	10	‡10
Pied (clear flighted varieties) ...	45	20	10	10	¶15
Pied (Recessive varieties)	45	20	‡20	—	‡15
Dark-eyed Clear varieties	45	20	35	—	—
Lacewings	45	20	10	10	15

* Points allocated for depth of colour and clearness of wings.
† Including clear mantle and neck (10 points). § Includes band.
‡ Including contrast in variegation.
¶ Including clear flights and tail.

Teams of 6 birds of any one colour or teams of 4 birds of any one colour. Points: General quality, 50. Uniformity, 50.

After these details of the ideal budgerigar and the Budgerigar Society's Scale of Points for each coloured variety we come to the Society's Colour Standards. These give an excellent description of the colours concerned and give a very full guide to the details. All those interested in these birds are indebted to the Society for producing these standards.

Two types of nest-boxes

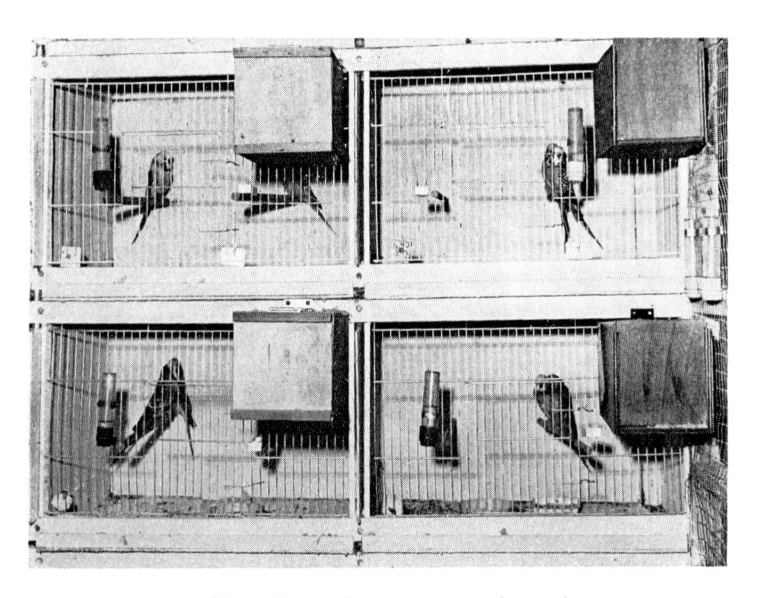

Control breeding pairs in cages and nest-boxes

(Above) The first four eggs out of seven. *(Below)* The first one out. A budgie chick of less than twelve hours old

(Above) The first chick is now seven days old and has company. *(Below)* There are four chicks here. The biggest is fifteen days old. The others are thirteen, eleven and nine days old

(Above) The chicks at the ages of twenty-four, twenty-two, twenty and eighteen days old and beginning to get their proper feathers. *(Below)* The oldest of these chicks is now five weeks old

THE BUDGERIGAR SOCIETY'S COLOUR STANDARDS

LIGHT GREEN

Mask, buttercup yellow, ornamented by six evenly spaced large round black throat spots, the outer two being partially covered at the base by cheek-patches. *Cheek Patches:* violet. *General body colour:* back, rump, breast, flanks and underparts, bright grass green of a solid and even shade throughout. *Markings:* on cheeks, back of head, neck and wings, black and well defined on a buttercup ground. *Tail:* long feathers, bluish black.

DARK GREEN

As above but with a dark laurel green body colour. *Tail:* long feathers, darker in proportion.

OLIVE GREEN

As above but with a deep olive green body colour. *Tail:* long feathers, darker in proportion.

GREY GREEN

The Grey Green conforms to the standard for Light Green except in the following details: *Cheek-patches:* grey to slate. *General body colour:* dull mustard green. *Tail:* long feathers, black. (It should be noted that there are light, medium and dark shades of Grey Green.)

LIGHT YELLOW

Mask: buttercup yellow. *Cheek-patches:* silvery white to very pale pinkish violet. *General body colour:* back, rump, breast, flanks and underparts, deep buttercup yellow and as free from green suffusion as possible. *Primaries and tail:* lighter than body. *Eye:* black pupil with white iris.

DARK YELLOW

Same as above but correspondingly deeper in colour.

OLIVE YELLOW

As above but with a mustard body colour.

GREY YELLOW

As above but with a dull mustard body colour. (It should be noted that there are light, medium and dark shades of Grey Yellow.)

SKYBLUE

Mask: clear white, ornamented by six evenly spaced large round black throat spots, the outer two being partially covered at the base by cheek-patches. *Cheek-patches:* violet. *General body colour:* back, rump, breast, flanks and underparts, pure skyblue. *Markings:* on cheeks, back of head, neck and wings, black and well defined on a white ground. *Tail:* long feathers, bluish black.

COBALT

As above but with a deep rich cobalt blue body colour. *Tail:* long feathers, darker in proportion.

MAUVE

As above but with a purplish mauve body colour with a tendency to a pinkish tone. *Tail:* long feathers, darker in proportion.

VIOLET

As above but with a deep intense violet body colour. *Tail:* long feathers, darker in proportion.

GREY

Mask: white, ornamented by six evenly spaced large round black throat spots, the outer two being partially covered at the base by cheek-patches. *Cheek-patches:* grey-blue or slate. *General body colour:* back, rump, breast, flanks and underparts, solid grey. *Markings:* on cheeks, back of head, neck and wings, black and well defined on a white ground. *Tail:* long feathers, black. (It should be noted that there are light, medium and dark shades of Grey.)

WHITE

Mask: white. *General body colour:* back, rump, breast, flanks and underparts, white (suffused with the colour being masked). *Wings and and tail:* white, bluish or light grey. (It should be noted that there are blue, cobalt, mauve, violet and grey shades in both light and dark suffusion.)

OPALINE LIGHT GREEN

Mask: buttercup yellow, extending over back of head and merging into general body colour at a point level with the butt of wings where undulations should cease thus leaving a clear V effect between top of wings so desirable in this variety, to be ornamented by six evenly spaced large round black throat spots, the outer two being partially covered at the base by cheek-patches. *Cheek-patches:* violet. *General body colour:* mantle (including V area or saddle), back, rump, breast, flanks and underparts, bright grass green. *Wings:* to be the same colour as body. *Markings:* should be normal with a suffused opalescent effect. *Tail:* long feathers, not to be lighter than mantle.

OPALINE DARK GREEN

As above but with a dark laurel green body colour. *Tail:* long feathers, not to be lighter than mantle.

OPALINE OLIVE GREEN

As above but with an olive green body colour: *Tail:* long feathers, not to be lighter than mantle.

OPALINE GREY GREEN

As above but with a dull mustard green body colour. *Tail:* long feathers, not to be lighter than mantle. *Cheek-patches:* grey to slate.

(It should be noted that there are light, medium and dark shades of Opaline Grey Green.)

OPALINE SKYBLUE

Mask: white, extending over back of head and merging into general body colour at a point level with the butt of wings where undulations should cease thus leaving a clear V effect between the top of wings so desirable in this variety, to be ornamented by six evenly spaced large round black throat spots, the outer two being partially covered at the base by cheek-patches. *Cheek-patches:* violet. *General body colour:* mantle (including V area or saddle), back, rump, breast, flanks and underparts, pure skyblue. *Wings:* to be the same colour as body. *Markings:* should be normal with a suffused opalescent effect. *Tail:* long feathers, not to be lighter than mantle.

OPALINE COBALT

As above but with a cobalt body colour. *Tail:* long feathers, not to be lighter than mantle.

OPALINE MAUVE

As above but with a mauve body colour. *Tail:* long feathers, not to be lighter than mantle.

OPALINE VIOLET

As above but with a deep intense violet body colour. *Tail:* long feathers, not to be lighter than mantle.

OPALINE GREY

As above but with a solid grey body colour. *Cheek-patches:* grey to slate. *Tail:* long feathers, no lighter than mantle. (It should be noted that there are light, medium and dark shades of Opaline Grey.)

OPALINE WHITE

As for White but with a suggestion of Opaline characteristics.

OPALINE YELLOW

As for Yellow but with a suggestion of Opaline characteristics.

OPALINE CINNAMON LIGHT GREEN

Mask: buttercup yellow, extending over back of head and merging into general body colour at a point level with butt of wings where undulations should cease, thus leaving a clear V effect between top of wings so desirable in this variety, to be ornamented by six evenly spaced large cinnamon brown throat spots; the outer two being partially covered at the base by cheek-patches. *Cheek-patches:* violet. *General body colour:* mantle (including V area or saddle), back, rump, breast, flanks and underparts, pale grass green. Wings to be same colour as body. *Markings:* should be normal cinnamon brown with a suffused opalescent effect. *Tail:* long feathers, not to be lighter than mantle.

OPALINE CINNAMON DARK GREEN

As above but with a light laurel green body colour. *Tail:* long feathers, not to be lighter than mantle.

OPALINE CINNAMON OLIVE GREEN

As above but with a light olive green body colour. *Tail:* long feathers, not to be lighter than mantle.

OPALINE CINNAMON GREY GREEN

As above but with a pale grey green body colour. *Tail:* long feathers, not to be lighter than mantle. *Cheek-patches:* grey to slate. (It should be noted that there are light, medium and dark shades of Opaline Cinnamon Grey Green.)

OPALINE CINNAMON SKYBLUE

Mask: white, extending over back of head and merging into general body colour at a point level with butt of wings where undulations should cease, thus leaving a clear V effect between top of wings so desirable in this variety; to be ornamented by six evenly spaced large round cinnamon brown throat spots, the outer two being partially covered at the base by cheek-patches. *Cheek-patches:* violet. *General body colour:* mantle, back, rump, breast, flanks and underparts, pale skyblue. *Markings:* should be normal cinnamon brown on pale blue ground with suffused opalescent effect. *Tail:* long feathers, not to be lighter than mantle.

OPALINE CINNAMON COBALT

As above but with pale cobalt body colour. *Tail:* long feathers, not to be lighter than mantle.

OPALINE CINNAMON MAUVE

As above but with pale mauve body colour. *Tail:* long feathers, not to be lighter than mantle.

OPALINE CINNAMON VIOLET

As above but pale violet body colour. *Tail:* long feathers, not to be lighter than mantle.

OPALINE CINNAMON GREY

As above but with pale grey body colour: *Cheek-patches:* grey to slate. *Tail:* long feathers, not to be lighter than mantle. (It should be noted that there are light, medium and dark shades of Opaline Cinnamon Grey.)

CINNAMON LIGHT GREEN

Mask: buttercup yellow, ornamented by six evenly spaced large round cinnamon brown throat spots the outer two being partially covered at the base by cheek-patches. *Cheek-patches:* violet. *General body colour:* back, rump, breast, flanks and underparts grass green, 50% or more of normal body colour. *Markings:* on cheeks, back of head, neck and wings, cinnamon brown on a yellow ground and distinct as in normal colour. *Tail:* long feathers, dark blue with brown quill.

CINNAMON DARK GREEN

As above but with a light laurel green body colour. *Tail:* long feathers, darker in proportion.

CINNAMON OLIVE GREEN

As above but with a light olive green body colour. *Tail:* long feathers, darker in proportion.

CINNAMON GREY GREEN

As above but with a pale grey green body colour. *Cheek-patches:* grey to slate. *Tail:* long feathers, of a deep cinnamon shade. (It should be noted that there are light, medium and dark shades of Cinnamon Grey Green.)

CINNAMON SKYBLUE

Mask: white, ornamented by six evenly spaced large round cinnamon brown throat spots, the outer two being partially covered at the base by cheek-patches. *Cheek-patches:* violet. *General body colour:* back, rump, breast, flanks and underparts skyblue 50% or more of normal body colour. *Markings:* cheeks, back of head, neck and wings cinnamon brown on white ground and distinct as in normal colour. *Tail:* long feathers, blue with brown quill.

CINNAMON COBALT

As above but with pale cobalt body colour. *Tail:* long feathers, cobalt with cinnamon shade.

CINNAMON MAUVE

As above but with pale mauve body colour. *Tail:* long feathers, mauve with cinnamon shade.

CINNAMON VIOLET

As above but with pale violet body colour. *Tail:* long feathers, violet with cinnamon shade.

CINNAMON GREY

As above but with pale grey body colour. *Cheek-patches:* pale grey. *Tail:* long feathers, pale grey with cinnamon shade. (It should be noted that there are light, medium and dark shades of Cinnamon Grey.)

GREYWING LIGHT GREEN

Mask: yellow, ornamented by six evenly spaced large round grey throat spots, the outer two being partially covered at the base by cheek-patches. *Cheek-patches:* pale violet. *General body colour:* back, rump, breast, flanks and underparts grass green 50% or more of normal body colour. *Markings:* on cheek, back of head, neck and wings should be light grey and distinct as in normal colour. *Tail:* long feathers, grey with pale bluish tinge.

GREYWING DARK GREEN

As above but with a light laurel green body colour. *Tail:* long feathers, darker in proportion.

GREYWING OLIVE GREEN

As above but with a light olive green body colour. *Tail:* long feathers, darker in proportion.

GREYWING GREY GREEN

As above but with a light mustard green body colour. *Cheek-patches:* light grey. *Tail:* long feathers, dark grey. (It should be noted that there are light, medium and dark shades of Greywing Grey Green.)

GREYWING SKYBLUE

Mask: white, ornamented by six evenly spaced large round grey throat spots, the outer two being partially covered at the base by cheek-patches. *Cheek-patches:* light violet. *General body colour:* back, rump, breast, flanks and underparts sky blue 50% or more of normal body colour. *Markings:* on cheek, back of head, neck and wings should be light grey and distinct as in normal colour. *Tail:* long feathers, greyish blue tinge.

GREYWING COBALT

As above but with a pale cobalt body colour. *Tail:* long feathers, darker in proportion.

GREYWING MAUVE

As above but with a pale mauve body colour. *Tail:* long feathers, darker in proportion.

GREYWING VIOLET

As above but with a pale violet body colour. *Tail:* long feathers, darker in proportion.

GREYWING GREY

As above but with a pale grey body colour. *Cheek-patches:* pale grey. *Tail:* long feathers, dark grey. (It should be noted that there are light, medium and dark shades of Greywing Grey.)

OPALINE GREYWING LIGHT GREEN

Mask: yellow extending over back of head and merging into general body colour at a point level with butt of wings where undulations should cease leaving a definite V effect between top of wings so desirable in this variety, to be ornamented by six evenly spaced large round grey throat spots, the outer two being partially covered at the base by cheek-patches. *Cheek-patches:* violet. *General body colour:* mantle (including V area or saddle), back, rump, breast, flanks and underparts, pale grass green. Wings same colour as body. *Markings:* should be normal and light grey in colour with suffused opalescent effect. *Tail:* long feathers, smoky grey

OPALINE GREYWING DARK GREEN

As above but with a light laurel green body colour. *Tail:* long feathers, darker in proportion.

OPALINE GREYWING OLIVE GREEN

As above but with a light olive green body colour. *Tail:* long feathers, darker in proportion.

OPALINE GREYWING GREY GREEN

As above but with a light mustard body colour. *Cheek-patches:* light grey. *Tail:* long feathers, dark grey. (It should be noted that there are light, medium and dark shades of Opaline Greywing Grey Green.)

OPALINE GREYWING SKYBLUE

Mask: white, extending over back of head and merging into general body colour at a point level with the butt of wings where undulations should cease leaving a definite clear V effect between top of wings so desirable in this variety, to be ornamented by six evenly spaced large round grey throat spots, the outer two being partially covered at the base by cheek-patches. *Cheek-patches:* violet. *General body colour:* mantle (including V area or saddle), back, rump, breast, flanks and underparts, pale skyblue. Wings same colour as body. *Markings:* should be normal and grey in colour with suffused opalescent effect. *Tail:* long feathers, grey.

OPALINE GREYWING COBALT

As above but with pale cobalt body colour. *Tail:* darker in proportion.

OPALINE GREYWING MAUVE

As above but with pale mauve body colour. *Tail:* darker in proportion.

OPALINE GREYWING VIOLET

As above but with pale violet body colour. *Tail:* darker in proportion.

OPALINE GREYWING GREY

As above but with pale grey body colour. *Cheek-patches:* light grey. *Tail:* long feathers, grey. (It should be noted that there are light, medium and dark shades of Opaline Greywing Grey.)

YELLOW-WING LIGHT GREEN

Mask: buttercup yellow. *Cheek-patches:* violet. *General body colour:* back, rump, breast, flanks and underparts, bright grass green. *Wings:* buttercup yellow, as free from markings as possible. *Tail:* long feathers, bluish.

YELLOW-WING DARK GREEN

As above but with dark laurel green body colour. *Tail:* long feathers, darker in proportion.

YELLOW-WING OLIVE GREEN

As above but with an olive green body colour. *Tail:* long feathers, darker in proportion.

YELLOW-WING GREY GREEN

This variety conforms to the standard for Yellow-wing Light Green except that general body colour should be dull mustard green. *Cheek-patches:* grey to slate. *Tail:* long feathers, darker in proportion. (It should be noted that there are light, medium and dark shades of Yellow-wing Grey Green.)

WHITEWING SKYBLUE

Mask: white. *Cheek-patches:* violet. *General body colour*: back, rump, breast, flanks and underparts, pure skyblue approximating to the normal variety. *Wings:* white, as free from markings as possible. *Tail:* long feathers, bluish.

WHITEWING COBALT

As above but with a cobalt body colour. *Tail:* long feathers, darker in proportion.

WHITEWING MAUVE

As above but with a mauve body colour. *Tail:* long feathers, darker in proportion.

WHITEWING VIOLET

As above but with a violet body colour. *Tail:* long feathers, darker in proportion.

WHITEWING GREY

As above but with a grey body colour. *Cheek-patches:* grey-blue. *Tail:* long feathers, grey. (It should be noted that there are light, medium and dark shades of Whitewing Grey.)

FALLOW LIGHT GREEN

Mask: yellow, ornamented by six evenly spaced large round brown throat spots, the outer two being partially covered at the base by cheek-patches. *Cheek-patches:* violet. *General body colour:* back, rump, breast, flanks and underparts, yellowish green. *Markings:* on cheeks, back of head, neck and wings, medium brown on a yellow ground. *Eyes:* red or plum. *Tail:* long feathers, bluish grey.

FALLOW DARK GREEN

As above but with a light laurel olive green body colour. *Tail:* long feathers, darker in proportion.

FALLOW OLIVE GREEN

As above but with a light mustard olive green body colour. *Tail:* long feathers, darker in proportion.

FALLOW GREY GREEN

As above but with a dull mustard green body colour. *Cheek-patches:* grey to slate. *Tail:* long feathers, darker in proportion. (It should be noted that there are light, medium and dark shades of Fallow Grey Green.)

FALLOW SKYBLUE

Mask: white, ornamented by six evenly spaced large round brown throat spots, the outer two being partially covered at base by cheek-patches. *Cheek-patches:* violet. *General body colour:* back, rump, breast, flanks and underparts, pale skyblue. *Markings:* on cheeks, back of head, neck and wings, medium brown on a white ground. *Eyes:* red or plum. *Tail:* long feathers, bluish grey.

FALLOW COBALT

As above but with a warm cobalt body colour. *Tail:* long feathers, darker in proportion.

FALLOW MAUVE

As above but with a pale mauve body colour of a pinkish tone. *Tail:* long feathers, darker in proportion.

FALLOW VIOLET

As above but with a pale violet body colour. *Tail:* long feathers, darker in proportion.

FALLOW GREY

As above but with a pale grey body colour. *Cheek-patches:* grey to slate. *Tail:* long feathers, darker in proportion. (It should be noted that there are light, medium and dark shades of Fallow Grey.) English and German forms are recognized; the German form having a white iris ring around the eye, the English form has none.

LUTINO

Buttercup yellow throughout. *Eyes:* clear red with light iris ring. *Cheek-patches:* silvery white. *Tail:* long feathers and primaries yellowish white.

ALBINO

White throughout. *Eyes:* clear red with light iris ring.

YELLOW-FACE

All varieties in the blue series except Pieds. *Mask:* yellow only, otherwise exactly as corresponding normal variety. Note: yellow-marked feathers in tail permissible.

PIEDS

DOMINANT PIED LIGHT GREEN

Mask: buttercup yellow of an even tone, ornamented by six evenly spaced and clearly defined large round black throat spots, the outer two being partially covered at the base by cheek-patches. *Cheek-patches:* violet. *General body colour:* as the normal Light Green variety but broken with irregular patches of clear buttercup yellow or with a clear yellow band approximately half an inch wide round its middle just above the thighs. An all yellow or normal green coloured body should be penalized. Head patch is optional. (Note: all other things being equal, preference to be given, in accordance with the scale of show points, to birds showing the band.) *Wings:* colour and markings as the normal Light Green but having irregular patches of clear buttercup yellow or with part of the wing edges to shoulder but clear yellow on an otherwise normal marked wing. Completely clear wings should be penalized. Wing markings may be grizzled in appearance. All visible flight feathers should be clear yellow but odd dark flight feathers are not faults. *Tail:* the two long tail feathers may be clear yellow, marked or normal blue-black in colour. *Cere:* similar to that of the normal Light Green or a mixture of normal colour and fleshy pink. *Eyes:* dark with light iris ring. *Beak:* normal horn colour. *Feet and legs:* blue mottled as the normal Light Green, fleshy pink or a mixture of both.

DOMINANT PIED DARK GREEN

As above but with general body colour as for normal Dark Green.

DOMINANT PIED OLIVE GREEN

As above but with general body colour as for normal Olive Green.

DOMINANT PIED GREY GREEN

As above but with general body colour as for normal Grey Green. *Cheek-patches:* grey-blue to slate. (It should be noted that there are light, medium and dark shades of Dominant Pied Grey Green.)

DOMINANT PIED SKYBLUE

Mask: white, ornamented by six evenly spaced and clearly defined large round black throat spots, the outer two being partially covered at the base by cheek-patches. *Cheek-patches:* violet. *General body colour:* as the normal Skyblue variety but broken with irregular patches of white or with a clear white band approximately half an inch wide round its middle just above the thighs. An all-white or normal blue coloured body should be penalized. Head-patch is optional. (Note: all other things being equal, preference to be given, in accordance with the scale of show points, to birds showing the band.) *Wings:* colour and markings as the normal Skyblue but having irregular patches of clear white or with part of the wing edges to shoulder but clear white on an otherwise normal marked wing. Completely clear wings should be penalized. Wing markings may be grizzled in appearance. All visible flight feathers should be clear white but odd dark feathers are not faults. *Tail:* the two long tail feathers may be clear white, marked or normal blue-black in colour. *Cere:* similar to that of normal Skyblue or a mixture of normal colour and fleshy pink. *Eyes:* dark with light iris ring. *Beak:* normal horn colour. *Feet and legs:* blue mottled as the normal Skyblue, fleshy pink or mixture of both.

DOMINANT PIED COBALT

As above but with general body colour as for normal Cobalt.

DOMINANT PIED MAUVE

As above but with general body colour as for normal Mauve.

DOMINANT PIED VIOLET

As above but with general body colour as for normal Violet.

DOMINANT PIED GREY

As above but with general body colour as for normal Grey. *Cheek-patches:* grey-blue or slate. (It should be noted that there are light, medium and dark shades of Dominant Pied Grey.) Note: an Opaline, Yellow-face and Cinnamon form of Dominent Pied is recognized but these should only be shown in Dominant Pied classes.

CLEARFLIGHT LIGHT GREEN

Mask: buttercup yellow of an even colour ornamented by six evenly spaced clearly defined large round black throat spots, the outer two being partially covered at the base by the cheek-patches. *Cheek-patches:* violet. *General body colour:* as the normal Light Green with the exception of one small patch approximately half an inch by five-eighths inch of clear buttercup yellow at the back of the head. Slight collar or extension of the bib, while undesirable, will not penalize. *Wings:* colour and markings as the normal Light Green but with seven visible flight feathers of clear yellow. Dark flights constitute a fault. *Tail:* the two long feathers should be clear yellow, dark tail feathers are a fault. *Cere:* similar to that of normal Light Green. *Eyes:* dark with light iris ring. *Beak:* normal horn colour. *Feet and legs:* blue mottled or flesh coloured.

CLEARFLIGHT DARK GREEN

As above but with general body colour as for normal Dark Green.

CLEARFLIGHT OLIVE GREEN

As above but with general body colour as for normal Olive Green.

CLEARFLIGHT GREY GREEN

As above but with general body colour as for normal Grey Green. *Cheek-patches:* grey blue or slate. (It should be noted that there are light, medium and dark shades of Pied (clear flighted) Grey Green.)

CLEARFLIGHT SKYBLUE

Mask: white, ornamented by six evenly spaced clearly defined large round black throat spots, the outer two being partially covered at the base by cheek-patches. *Cheek-patches:* violet. *General body colour:* as the normal Skyblue with the exception of one small patch approximately half-inch by five-eighths inch of pure white at the back of the head. Slight collar or extension of bib, while undesirable, will not penalize. *Wings:* as normal Skyblue but with seven visible flight feathers of pure white. Dark flights constitute a fault. *Tail:* the two long feathers should be pure white, marked or dark tail feathers are a fault. *Cere:* similar to that of normal Skyblue. *Eyes:* dark with light iris ring. *Beak:* normal horn colour. *Feet and legs:* bluish mottled or flesh colour.

CLEARFLIGHT COBALT

As above but with general body colour as for normal Cobalt.

CLEARFLIGHT MAUVE

As above but with general body colour as for normal Mauve.

CLEARFLIGHT VIOLET

As above but with general body colour as for normal Violet.

CLEARFLIGHT GREY

As above but with general body colour as for normal Grey. *Cheek-patches:* grey-blue to slate. (It should be noted that there are light, medium and dark shades of Clearflight Grey.)

Note: An Opaline, Yellow-face and Cinnamon form of Clearflight is recognized but these should only be shown in Clearflight classes. The non-head-spot type of Clearflight (described as Australian) with full body colour is recognized and should be exhibited in Clearflight classes where these are provided.

DARK-EYED CLEAR YELLOW

Cheek-patches: silvery-white. *General body colour:* pure yellow throughout and free from any odd green feathers or green suffusion. *Wings:* pure yellow throughout, free from black or grizzled tickings or green suffusion. All flight feathers paler yellow than rump colour. *Tail:* as the flight feathers. *Cere:* fleshy pink in colour as in Lutinos. *Eyes:* dark without any light iris ring. *Beak:* orange coloured. *Feet and legs:* fleshy pink. (Note: the actual body colour varies in depth according to the genetical make-up, i.e. whether light, dark or olive green, etc.)

DARK-EYED CLEAR WHITE

As above but with white body colour and free from any blue suffusion or odd blue feathers. *Flights and tail:* white. *Cere:* fleshy pink in colour as in Albinos.

(Note: a dominant form is also recognized having normal cere, eyes, beak, feet and legs, which may be exhibited with the above-mentioned types of dark-eyed yellows and/or whites where separate classes are scheduled for this variety. A yellow-faced form of dark-eyed clear is also recognized but these should only be shown in Dark-eyed Clear classes.)

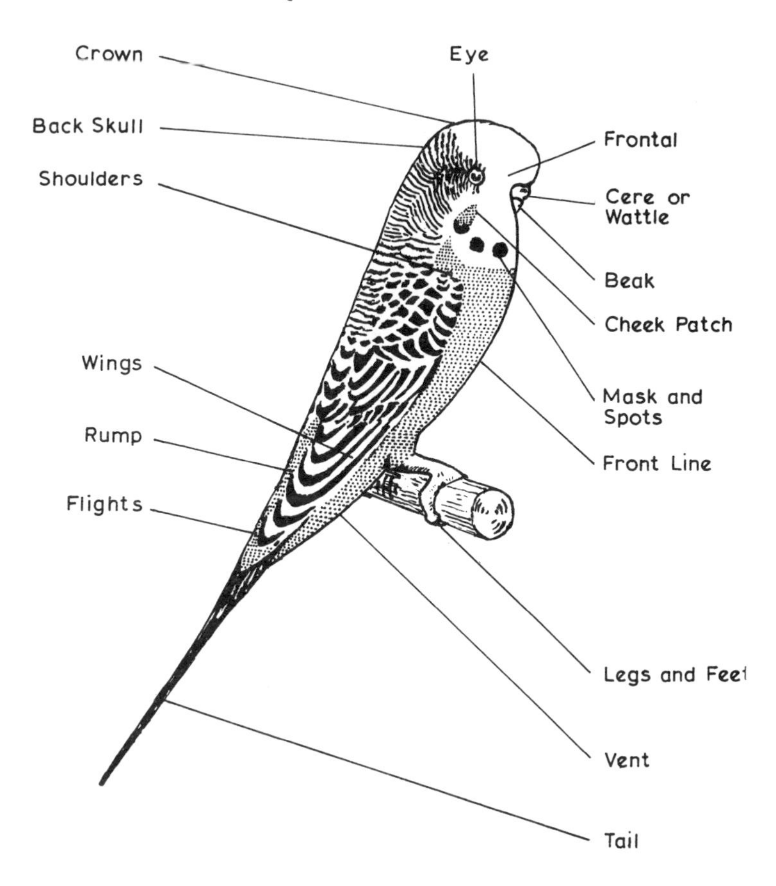

Principal Points of a Budgerigar

RECESSIVE PIED LIGHT GREEN

Mask: buttercup yellow of an even tone. *Throat spots:* as the normal Light Green variety, may be present from one to full number. *Cheek-patches:* violet, silvery-white or a mixture of both. *General body colour:* irregular patches of clear buttercup yellow and bright grass green with the latter mainly on the lower chest, rump and underparts. Zebra markings on the top of the head and around the eyes are not faults. *Wings:* black undulations or polka-dot markings should not cover more than fifteen to twenty per cent of total area. All visible flight feathers should be clear yellow but odd dark flight feathers are not faults. *Cere:* fleshy pink in colour as in Lutinos. *Eyes:* dark without any light iris ring. *Beak:* orange coloured. *Feet and legs:* fleshy pink.

RECESSIVE PIED DARK GREEN

As above but with a yellow and dark green body colour.

RECESSIVE PIED OLIVE GREEN

As above but with a yellow and olive green body colour.

RECESSIVE PIED GREY GREEN

As above but with a yellow and grey-green body colour. *Cheek-patches:* grey-blue or slate, or a mixture of both. (It should be noted that there are light, medium and dark shades of Recessive Pied Grey Green.)

RECESSIVE PIED SKYBLUE

Mask: white. *Throat spots:* as the normal Skyblue variety, may be present from one to full number. *Cheek-patches:* violet, silvery-white or a mixture of both. *General body colour:* irregular patches of white and bright skyblue with the latter mainly on the lower chest, rump and underparts. Zebra markings on top of head and around the eyes are not faults. *Wings:* black undulations or polka-dot markings should not cover more than fifteen to twenty per cent of total area. All visible flight feathers should be white but odd dark flight feathers are not faults. *Cere:* fleshy pink in colour as in Albinos. *Eyes:* dark without any light iris ring. *Beak:* orange coloured. *Feet and legs:* fleshy pink.

RECESSIVE PIED COBALT

As above but with a white and cobalt body colour.

RECESSIVE PIED MAUVE

As above but with a white and mauve body colour.

RECESSIVE PIED VIOLET

As above but with a white and violet body colour.

RECESSIVE PIED GREY

As above but with a white and grey body colour. *Cheek-patches:*

grey-blue or slate, or a mixture of both. (It should be noted that there are light, medium and dark forms of Recessive Pied Grey.)

Note: an Opaline, Yellow face and Cinnamon form of Recessive Pied is recognized but these should be shown only in Recessive Pied Classes.

LACEWING YELLOW

Mask: yellow, ornamented by six evenly spaced large round cinnamon throat spots, the outer two being partially covered at the base by cheek-patches. *Cheek-patches:* pale violet. *General body colour:* back, rump, breast, flanks and underparts, yellow. *Markings:* on cheeks, back of head, neck mantle and wings, cinnamon brown on a yellow ground. *Eyes:* clear red with light iris rings. *Tail:* long feathers, cinnamon brown. Note: the depth of yellow of the body colour, etc., varies according to the normal counterpart being masked by the Lacewing character, i.e. the richest yellow is carried by the Lacewing Olive Green and the lightest by the Lacewing Light Green.

LACEWING WHITE

Mask: white, ornamented by six evenly spaced large round cinnamon throat spots, the outer two being partially covered at the base by cheek-patches. *Cheek-patches:* pale violet. *General body colour:* back, rump, breast, flanks and underparts, white. *Markings:* on cheeks, back of head, neck, mantle and wings, cinnamon brown on a white ground. *Eyes:* clear red with light iris rings. *Tail:* long feathers, cinnamon brown. Note: the shade of white of the body colour etc., varies only slightly in tone according to the normal counterpart being masked by the lacewing character. (A yellow-faced form is recognized. Where no classes are scheduled for this variety it should be shown in any other colour classes.)

NINE

Ailments and Injuries

Although this chapter is on ailments and injuries, this has not been written because the average budgie is an unhealthy creature or because it is prone to injury. As with every living creature, there are always those that do happen to become sick or injured; but such is the natural robustness of these birds, that many go through their entire life without ailing in any way.

Nevertheless, as this book has been written to enlighten those who keep, or wish to keep, budgies, I feel it would be appropriate to mention most of the conditions that these birds can suffer, although, as I have already stated, very few ever do.

Most of the conditions are of a minor nature, but in every case prompt treatment is necessary, so I hope these remarks will assist you to deal quickly with a complaint, or help you to realize when a veterinary surgeon is needed.

SCALY-FACE

This is a complaint peculiar to budgies, and, as the name of the disease suggests, affects the face of the bird. It is in fact a form of skin complaint. The skin around the beak becomes fungoid, having a dry 'scurfy' scaly appearance. If neglected it could spread from the beak to

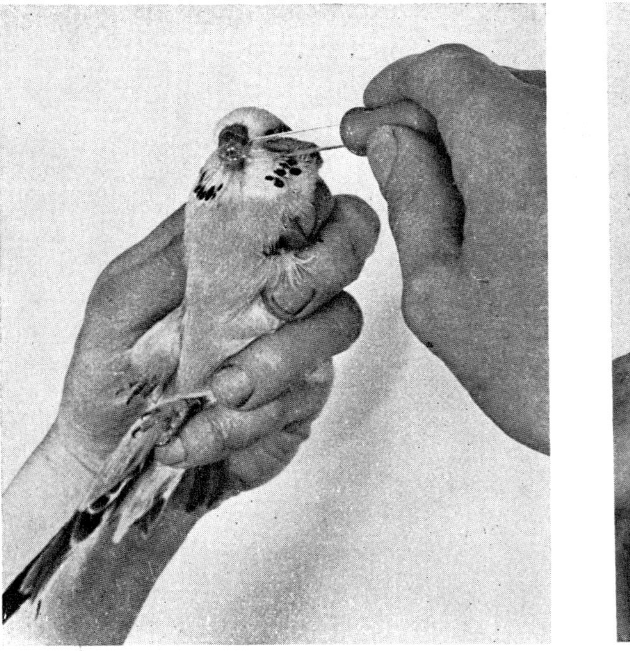

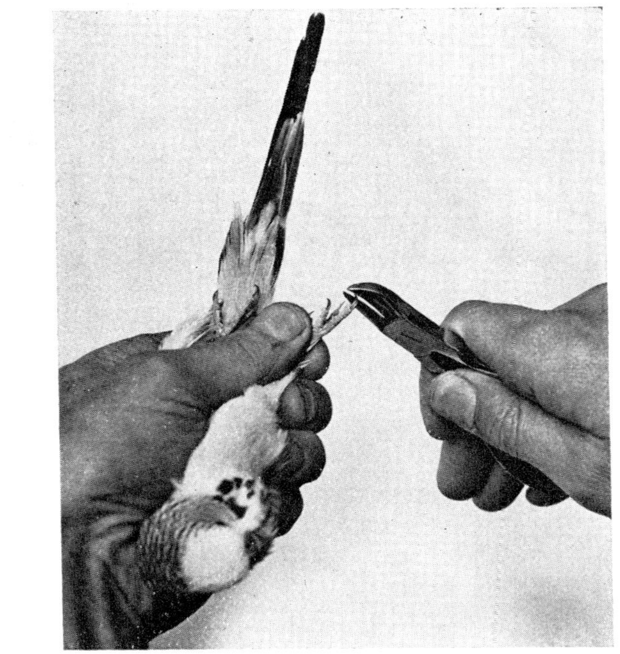

(Left) A budgie being given medicine with a dropper. *(Right)* A budgie's claws being trimmed

A spacious outside flight. Normally more budgies are on view, but it is the breeding season and only spare birds are to be seen

the head and eyes. Although I have seen cases as bad as this, it is very, very rare.

When a budgie first has this, it just looks as if the feathers are slightly sticking out around the beak, and often a budgie will have scaly-face for some time before the owner will even notice that there is anything wrong, although naturally in more severe cases it is more obvious.

Should your pet get this, there is no need for real concern, as this is really what can be classed as a 'nuisance' complaint, and with the right treatment can usually be cleared up in three or four weeks.

You can take your bird to a veterinary surgeon, who will prescribe something for it, or there are some excellent preparations which can be obtained from pet stores purely for treating this disorder. I have used these and found them successful in curing this ailment.

But whatever preparation you treat your pet with, always see that plently is put on the actual scaly-skin as you must completely kill the germ, otherwise this irritating malady will continue to remain on the bird's face. When you are about to treat the bird, move the feathers away from its beak and you will notice little sores which look like hard 'crusty' pimples. This is where the germ lives. It it is considered that scaly-face is caused by very small mites getting under the skin, so it is essential that the pimples and the surrounding skin are really saturated with the ointment or cream when you put it on.

Usually after a couple of treatments the scaly-face will begin to diminish. One of the reasons why this complaint often does not respond to treatment as quickly as it should is that the cage and the perches are are not cleaned as often as necessary. Scaly-face is contagious. When a bird has this, it often feels irritation in the face, and to relieve this rubs itself against the cage and perches and so infects them. If they are not washed regularly the bird will (even though it is being treated) continue to have this infection, so you will understand how important it is regularly to disinfect the cage and perches. A harmless disinfectant is a bowl of nearly boiling water with a handful of ordinary household soda dissolved in it. This will be excellent for the purpose, but when washing the cage it would be wise to use a piece of cloth that can be burnt after use to prevent further infection. Once the scaly-face has been cured, it is still a sound policy to wash the perches once a week.

I have written a lot about this complaint, which perhaps gives the impression that it is a serious one. This is not so, it is just a simple skin disease which, as I have stated previously, can be cured quite quickly if treated correctly. In addition, we do not wish our pets to look less than their best and scaly-face does not look very attractive.

Strangely enough, scaly-face does not seem to affect the bird's general health, other than causing irritation.

SPRAINS

The budgie when healthy is the most active of birds, forever on the move, continuously clambering here and jumping there, and so it sometimes happens that these lovable rascals have a minor mishap, perhaps a slip or a fall whilst climbing excitedly around, and they sprain a leg. This could appear quite serious at the time, but unless the bird has broken its leg (this is very rare and would cause it to have an unnatural, out-of-shape look, in which case it should be taken to a veterinary surgeon or animal treatment clinic) the sprain will usually get well within a few days. For some reason leg injuries in birds usually heal quickly; but you can help to hasten its recovery by lowering the perches in the cage. Even when a bird is badly hurt it will still attempt to get to its usual perch, so, by placing this lower, you can help to prevent the bird from aggravating the injury. Once the bird is well again the perches can be replaced to their normal positions.

For sprains the treatment which I have found beneficial is to rub the leg gently with warm olive-oil. This increases the blood flow and generally assists the leg to recover.

Whilst a bird has a bad leg (due to any cause) our aim should be to see that the bird has not got to use it more than necessary, so its seed, water, grit and any tit-bits should be placed on the floor so that it has easy access to them without having to climb. Lastly, should your bird hurt itself and not appear to be any better in a day or so, get a veterinary surgeon or animal clinic to look at it.

CONSTIPATION

Although this is not an ailment common to budgies, it nevertheless does seem to occur with an occasional bird and, although easy to treat, can be distressing both to the patient and its owner, who becomes upset watching his pet in this state, without knowing what to do.

When a bird is constipated it frequently strains itself trying to pass its motion, making jerking movements to try to eject its droppings, with very little success. If it has been constipated for any length of time, the vent (back passage) often becomes sore and irritated, and the patient will often attempt to pick at this to relieve itself.

First, we should attempt to ease the irritation around the vent by washing this with a warm wet cloth. This will often loosen any excreta which has stuck to the vent and give the bird immediate relief. Having washed it, wipe this dry with another piece of cloth (throw the pieces of used cloth away) and after this dust over the area washed with boracic powder. This is a wonderful soother and healer.

I have found Glauber's Salts very effective for the actual constipation. These salts can be purchased very cheaply from any chemist and are usually obtained in small crystals. Put a piece an eighth the size of a garden pea in the bird's drinking water, and if your bird drinks some of this it should get relief in a few hours. As it begins to pass its motions normally, repeat this dose for a day or so, until your pet is its usual self again.

After this I would advise you to put Glauber's Salts (dose as previously mentioned) in your pet's drinking water about once a month, leaving it in the cage for a day and thoroughly washing out the drinker the next. This, and greenfood or a piece of apple (not to be given on the same day as the Glauber's Salts) should help to keep your pal in good trim.

BLEEDING

I am mentioning bleeding as there are few living things which do not cut or knock themselves at some time or another, and budgies are no exception. I have seen birds bleeding badly, but I have never known them to suffer from any after-effects once the bleeding has stopped, provided there has not been any additional injury. Nevertheless bleeding can upset and cause great concern to the owner—often more in fact than it does to the patient.

Birds will often bleed quite freely even if there is very little injury. This particularly applies when the beak or claws are hurt.

Fortunately, in most cases, the bleeding can easily be stopped. I have found two remedies which are highly effective, both of which are commonly kept in the average household; they are tincture of iodine and Friar's Balsam.

Should you have to treat your bird for bleeding (quite possibly you will never have to), just wipe the affected part as dry as you can with a piece of cotton-wool or cloth, then pour either iodine or Friar's Balsam on to another piece of cotton-wool or cloth until it is reasonably wet, and hold it over the part which is bleeding for about a minute. Doing this will usually stop the bleeding immediately, although a second application might be necessary.

Bleeding often makes an injury look much worse than it actually is. You should remember this and calmly try to stop the bleeding. If this cannot be done promptly, take the bird to a veterinary surgeon or animal treatment clinic, but, as I have already stated, often it is a case of a very minor injury, with a lot of bleeding.

NIGHT-FRIGHT

This is something that may happen to a budgie, and, although it is not a complaint, many owners feel concerned over it and think their pet is suffering from some mental ailment. This is not so; it is just a case of a bird becoming frightened at night.

I mention night-fright, not because it is a common occurrence with budgies (in fact I have known fanciers who have kept these birds for years and have never experienced it), but so that, should you ever witness your pet in this frightened state, you will know what to do and not be worried by it.

Night-fright is similar to a human being's nightmare, and, like a nightmare, once it is over leaves no ill effects.

Budgies suffer night-fright through being startled in the dark. Perhaps it is asleep and a car door is slammed just outside, or a cat (which someone forgot to shut out) is in the room with the bird and suddenly moves. Possibly the curtains in the room have not been drawn over and the lights of passing cars dazzle the bird as they shine into the cage. The poor thing becomes startled and, being half asleep, jumps off its perch or place where it is roosting and begins to fly in its cage. (We should remember that a budgie is 'blind' when in the dark.) It cannot find a perch and so panics more and more and flies around the cage in an hysterical fashion.

Should you find your budgie in this state you will notice that as soon as the light is switched on it will go to the bottom of the cage with its wings outstretched as if collapsed. Let the bird stay in this condition with the light on for at least ten minutes before doing anything. During this time it should begin to wake up and become steadier. After waiting, gently speak to the bird and gradually encourage it to regain its senses and get back to its perch or roosting place. Once you are confident that it has completely calmed down, you can go to bed reassured that it will sleep and be its usual happy self in the morning.

Just a little advice to help to avoid your pet having night-fright. Always see that it is on the perch or place where it sleeps before putting out the light. If it is on the bottom of the cage and it suddenly becomes dark, it will not know where it is and will sometimes panic. So with this condition prevention is the best cure.

INJURED SKIN

Sometimes a budgie will catch its leg against a wire whilst climbing around in the cage, and, although the skin is not broken, it will leave a nasty scratch, which will sometimes fester if not treated.

A pet which has sustained this sort of injury should have the affected part bathed with warm water, then thoroughly dried with a towel. A little Friars Balsam or Vaseline should be smeared over it. This should heal the skin quickly.

GROWTHS AND LUMPS

Although growths are not common amongst budgies I have known them develop, and should a growth or lump begin to appear on your bird you should consult a veterinary surgeon immediately. He will be able to tell you whether it can be removed or cured by treatment. Growths should be treated only by veterinary surgeons.

I have been asked to look at budgies which have had growths, and in every case their owners assume that their treasured pet would have to be 'put to sleep'. I am pleased to say that in many cases I have been able to assure them that a veterinary surgeon would be able to remove the growth without detriment to the bird's health.

Sometimes it is not possible to treat a growth when it is growing internally, but those which are more or less on the outside of the bird's body can usually be removed successfully. To confirm this, during the last two years I have known of two birds which have had a 'fleshy' lump removed from one of their wings, and in another case a growth was removed from a budgie's neck. At the time of writing this, all three are alive and well.

So if you suspect your pet has a growth do not hesitate to consult a veterinary surgeon, as the earlier it is treated the better is the chance of success.

IRRITATION DUE TO LICE

On rare occasions I have come across a budgie that has lice on it. These small mites can cause great irritation, and so the bird will continuously pick and scratch at its feather to relieve the irritation. However, we must not confuse a bird preening itself with one which has lice and is irritated, and we should realize that perfectly clean and healthy birds often preen themselves to keep their feathers in good order.

They do this by rubbing their beak over a gland which is situated at the rump (the top of the tail). When this is done the gland discharges a fluid on to the bird which it then spreads over its feathers, giving that lovely glossy plumage that we see in a healthy specimen.

If your pet has lice and is obviously ill at ease through irritation, treatment these days is very simple. Aerosol spray preparations made for birds which have lice or feather irritation have recently become available. These have a double advantage over the other method of treatment, which is to rub powder into the bird's feathers, as with the spray there is no need to 'catch' the patient to put it on, and whilst you are spraying the bird you can also spray the cage, killing any lice that may be lurking there. When you use the spray always be sure to remove the seed, water, grit and cuttlefish bone first, naturally replacing them a short while after the spraying has been done.

Also, to assist your bird to have good plumage, give your pet an opportunity to have a bath when the weather is not too cold. After all the biggest enemy of lice is cleanliness.

ASTHMA (WHEEZING)

It is not often that this is found in budgies (it is more prevalent in canaries) but, like asthma in humans, it is often difficult to cure. From my experience with birds which have suffered with wheezing and shortness of breath, it is essential that they are kept in the right environment to bring about relief, as this complaint is aggravated by low temperatures, and unless the room is kept warm constantly, the sufferer could become fatally ill.

I have observed that budgies born and reared in cold aviaries rarely, if ever, suffer from this, whereas those brought up in less hardy circumstances often become asthmatic in cold weather when kept in cold quarters.

To assist a pet suffering from asthma see that it is kept in a reasonably warm room, and at nights place a thin cloth over the top of the cage—but please not so tight that the poor creature finds it difficult to breathe.

For treatment there are several veterinary preparations that can be tried. Sometimes five drops of tincture of iodine placed in the bird's drinking water will prove beneficial, and on occasions when I have had birds which were really ill, I have mixed two drops of brandy (medical drops, not spirit measure drops) with one tablespoonful of luke-warm water and given it to the bird either by means of a dropper or by placing in the drinker. This will bring relief, but we should bear in mind that asthmatic birds should not be given medicine direct unless it is as a last resort, as too much exertion can be dangerous to the bird.

We should remember at this time, or at any time when a bird is sick, whether it is with asthma, a chill, or stomach disorder, that it is essential we should induce our pet to eat (although it may not feel much like doing so) in order to keep it alive. At times like this I have found millet sprays invaluable, as even a sick bird will often peck at these when nothing else will tempt it.

With asthma, the best results can be obtained by seeing that the patient remains in a constant, warm atmosphere. This should also ensure that these spasms will not recur.

When the bird recovers (very few die with this if treated promptly) see that it is given, every other day or so, a piece of greenfood such as clean, frost-free chickweed, seeding grass, lettuce, cabbage or spinach. Should it be frosty weather a piece of apple will do.

Also ensure that only the barest minimum of perches and toys are in the cage, so that the bird has ample room to move, as asthma is more often associated with pets that are obese than with thin ones.

CHILLS

Budgies can suffer with chills, just like humans. Treatment for this is mainly warmth, and brandy could be given as prescribed for asthma or wheezing. A chill will usually pass off in a few days if the bird is kept in the right temperature, but even if the patient appears quite well, care should be taken to see that the bird is not placed suddenly in a cold room after it has been in the warmth, as this could cause a relapse. Luckily most pet birds have heat available during the cold spells, and the chill is usually caused by the draught from a door which has accidentally been left open, so please see that your pet is placed out of draughts.

CLAWS AND BEAKS

Although budgies might have claws which need trimming, or perhaps a beak that grows and therefore needs cutting back occasionally, these are not ailments in the ordinary sense of the word. However, if claws and beaks are neglected (and they often are, through an owner's ignorance or lack of thought), this can lead to a bird being disabled. If its claws are allowed to grow too long and twisted the bird can become virtually a cripple, being unable either to walk or climb properly.

Likewise, a bird with an overlong beak will not be able to eat with ease. So you see it is important that owners should look regularly at their pet's feet and beaks to see all is well. Budgies' claws usually need trimming every six months or so—although every bird varies, some needing trimming more often than this, whilst others have claws which hardly seem to grow at all.

Trimming, although not a difficult task to an expert, can be tricky to the inexperienced, so if at all possible get an experienced person to do it for you, at least for the first time, so that you can see how it is done.

One of the secrets of cutting claws is to hold the bird so that its legs do not move whilst the nails are actually being trimmed, or the patient might be cut elsewhere. Secondly, never cut the nail too close. It is much wiser to trim off a little at a time and do it more often. Cutting too close might cut into the vein, causing bleeding. Should this ever occur when you are trimming your pet's claws, or through the bird accidentally breaking a nail, put some tincture of iodine or Friars Balsam on to a cloth and hold over the claw for a minute or so. This will normally stop the bleeding. If you hold a budgie's foot up to the light you can see where the vein or artery ends in each claw. No harm will come if you trim well clear of it.

The reason why some budgies have beaks that grow is one of nature's mysteries. There is a theory that these birds were under-nourished when very young due to their parents being poor feeders. This could be one of the reasons, but it is not always when the bird is young that the beak grows. One bird I owned was a prize-winner and had a perfectly shaped beak until it was five years old, and then for no apparent reason its beak began to grow very quickly. Until it died at the age of nine I had to cut its beak as often as every two months, and this bird had the most nourishing diet available.

To conclude, it is quite possible that your budgie's

claws will grow constantly and will therefore have to be trimmed regularly, but with regards to its beak, it is unlikely that it will ever grow. Should it do so, however, take it to some experienced person to have it cut as, although it is not a delicate operation, it should not be performed by anyone inexperienced, unless they have been shown how to do so by an expert.

STOMACH UPSETS

The budgie is by nature inquisitive, it likes to feel and taste things that it comes in contact with, and this desire to bite at objects can sometimes lead to a tummy-upset. It might have bitten something off its cage or eaten a piece of stale greenfood which had been left in the cage from yesterday. (This should always be removed the same day that it is given, before it has become withered.) Then poor Joey, although not looking really ill, looks out-of-sorts and is not as lively as usual. His droppings will be looser than normal, although not resembling the motion of a bird suffering from true enteritis, when they come away from the sick bird like water. Fortunately true enteritis rarely affects budgies, but as it might occur I will deal with this complaint in more detail later in the chapter.

Knowing your bird is unwell and its stomach is affected, you should remove the grit from its cage and refrain from giving greenfood, as this will aggravate the condition. Throw away the seed which is in the cage, wash the pot out and fill with new seed, as often old dusty seed can cause digestive upsets.

At this time (or any time when a pet is sick with stomach upsets, chills or asthma) the first essential is to see that the sufferer is in a constant warm temperature and away from draughts. This means that the bird can use its energy to fight the illness instead of using it to keep itself warm, as it would have to if left in the cold. A cloth around the back and sides of the cage will assist in keeping the inmate in an even temperature. Heat should never be excessive, but warm enough to do good.

Having seen that our pet is warm, we can begin the treatment. There are several medicines which can be obtained at pet stores for this, in both liquid and powder form. Although we can put the liquid into water for the bird to drink, or the powder on its seed for it to take, sometimes a 'patient' will not eat or drink for some time, and, as prompt treatment is necessary, I think it advisable that the first dose should always be given to the bird direct. We can then be sure that it has had its medicine and should begin to benefit from it immediately.

If liquid is to be inserted into the mouth, a dropper is fine for this purpose, always of course ensuring that the bird is given the correct dose as prescribed. But if you wish to give powder direct, a matchstick pared at one end to make it wider and flatter, will prove ideal. This sort of matchstick will hold sufficient powder for you to put into the bird's beak and give the required dose. The great advantage with using matchsticks is that after each use they can be burnt, thus lessening the chance of further infection.

If you have kept the patient warm and given it the appropriate medicine it should begin to look brighter in a few hours. We then know that all is well, although we should continue to keep it warm and see that it has further medicine. If it seems worse do not let it go on in this state, ask a veterinary surgeon to look at it.

ACUTE ENTERITIS

As I have previously stated, this very serious complaint

is uncommon amongst budgies, and during the number of years that I have kept these wonderful birds, I have only known of three true cases of enteritis.

This complaint requires the attention of a veterinary surgeon immediately as, even with this troublesome disorder, the new wonder drugs can perform marvels.

The symptoms of a patient with acute enteritis is that it looks bad and all 'fluffed-up'. Its tail flicks up and down incessantly as it breathes, it vomits freely from the mouth, and the excreta (droppings) become greeny and very loose (sometimes coming from the bird like water) and smell very strongly.

Assuming the patient is now being treated for this complaint, you also have a very important part to play to assist in the bird's ultimate recovery.

As acute enteritis is infectious and cleanliness is a vital necessity in fighting it, you should start by thoroughly washing the perches, making certain they are dry before replacing them. If the bird is very sick do not disturb it unduly, by removing the perch it is on, but put the clean perches into the cage and when it goes onto one of these remove the infected odd perch and wash it like the others replacing when dry. It is important that all perches are dry when a bird is sick, as an ailing bird will become even worse if it has to sit on wet perches. Next remove the tray and, if there is one, the loose bottom of the cage and wash with boiling water which has had a handful of common household soda added to it. This will act as an ideal disinfectant without harming the bird. Whilst the bird is sick with this disorder the tray should be washed daily as this will help considerably to eradicate the infection. (It is wise to destroy the cloth used for cleaning if the bird has any infectious complaint.)

The patient should begin to improve in a few days with

the right treatment, but it is important at this time to remember that, although it will look better, it will still be very weak, and should remain in a warm atmosphere for some time. If this is not done the patient is likely to suffer with a chill and become very ill again.

I have written about enteritis knowing that, out of the millions of budgies kept, very few will ever suffer from it; but should you ever suspect that your pet has enteritis, do not hesitate to ask a veterinary surgeon to look at it.

FOOD REGURGITATION

I am writing about this, not because it is a disease (far from it!) but because to those who are inexperienced with budgies this action is looked upon as such.

Regurgitating is when a bird, after having swallowed and digested its food, brings it up again. When owners see this they naturally assume their pet is sick—which is quite understandable, as elsewhere in this chapter I have mentioned that vomiting is a symptom of enteritis. However, when a bird vomits through sickness, it will look very 'sorry' for itself and really out of sorts, whereas if it is naturally regurgitating, it is the complete reverse, in fact it is in 'fighting-fit' condition.

Perhaps I should explain further. At breeding time, if a cock bird is healthy when he is paired to the hen, he will automatically regurgitate his food and feed her. This assists both birds to attain peak breeding condition.

Once the eggs are laid, if the hen is a good breeder she will rarely leave the nest-box. During this period the cock will feed her, and will continue to do so when the young hatch. She will then feed the chicks, and often the male bird will assist in feeding the brood.

So you see that when a bird regurgitates its food it is in natural breeding condition and healthy.

Perhaps some of you who are reading this are thinking: "How can I tell if my pet is vomiting because it is sick, or regurgitating because it is in breeding condition?"

The answer is simple—by the way it acts! If it is suffering from a serious stomach disorder, it would look lifeless, puffed-out and mopey, often spending a lot of time with its head under its wing, and generally looking unwell. If, however, it regurgitates through being in breeding condition, it will be the opposite—full of life, constantly jumping about the cage, continuously 'chattering' and perhaps feeding its mirror or bell, or something else in its cage, and showing every sign of being on top of the world.

I have known owners who have been very distressed to see their bird regurgitating, but I can assure you there is no reason to feel this way. If your pet is healthy and regurgitates it is only performing a perfectly natural function. If the bird had a mate it would have fed her, but, as it has not, it regurgitates and feeds the bell in the cage etc., during this breeding phase. When the breeding desire ceases the regurgitation stops, so please don't think it is anything to worry about. When a budgie acts like this it is in the pink of condition.

OBESITY

Obesity, or fatness, is not an ailment in itself, but can lead to poor health. I would like to say right away, however, that no bird, whether it is fat or not, should be put on a diet. Budgies are not like humans, they only eat the quantity they require, and it is my opinion that most birds which are over-fat are like this because of some fault in the way they are kept. Obesity in most cases is due to lack of exercise, and many obese pets that I have seen have never exercised much because they have never had the opportunity. Just imagine how you would feel if you were kept in a lovely room, which was unfortunately so full of furniture that you could hardly move, and when you did try to move or jump, you just knocked and hurt yourself. Eventually you would never jump and rarely move, and so become fat and unwell.

Sadly, many birds are in this situation, they live in a lovely cage, but unfortunately there is so much paraphernalia inside it (bells, ladders, toys, swings, etc.,) that they can hardly move, and so become obese and listless. So if your bird seems a bit too fat, have a good look at what is inside its cage. A couple of perches and a swing is all that is usually necessary. Take out most of the other things and I am certain that in a few weeks you will have a lot livelier pet—and a thinner one too!

EGG-BINDING

This is a distressing complaint that can sometimes occur in breeding hens—although fortunately this does not happen to many—and as the name implies, infers that the bird is unable to lay or pass its egg.

There is no mistaking when a hen is egg-bound. The poor thing will be lying either on the floor of the cage or, less usually, in the nest-box, looking in a sorry state, with her feathers ruffled-up and her wings slightly outstretched. Her tail will be flicking as she tries in vain to pass the offending egg.

From my experience with egg-bound hens, although all of them will look the same when you first find them in this condition, and will need heat to assist them, there are two sorts of ailment. One is of a minor nature and fortunately is much more common than acute egg-binding.

The less severe egg-binding appears to be caused by a form of cramp (sometimes cold conditions seems to bring this on) which prevents the hen from using the muscles that function to expel the egg.

I have found that to give brandy and water (two medicine drops of brandy to one teaspoonful of water) without delay is always beneficial to egg-bound hens. You should then spread a little warm olive-oil around the vent, with a feather as the application must be done gently. Then place the bird in an hospital cage, or a box-type cage placed near a fire, not too near so as to burn or to cause discomfort to it, but close enough for the occupant to really feel the warmth for an hour or so. In minor forms of egg-binding this will be sufficient to enable the patient to lay her egg.

Sometimes, after we have tried the course of treatment just described, it is obvious after an hour or so, that the hen is still in distress and cannot lay the egg through her own efforts. This is due perhaps to the egg being mis-shaped or soft-shelled which causes it to become elongated as the hen puts pressure on it to pass it.

Then other measures must be taken. Before you start these, you should give the bird a further dose of brandy and water, giving this as previously with either a dropper or small spoon direct into the beak. You should then put the hen back into the cage again and allow a few minutes for the brandy to have a strengthening effect.

Whilst you are waiting for the brandy to help the patient, you should find some petroleum jelly, a piece of muslin or thin cloth, and a narrow necked jug or vase, as you will need these for further treatment for the bird.

You should then heat some water almost to boiling point, and put it into a jug or vase. Then place the cloth over the top of it. Taking the bird from its cage, place a little petroleum jelly around its vent (this is to prevent the steam from scalding it). Having done this, hold the bird over the container and allow the steam to come up to the vent of the hen for a few seconds. Sometimes you might need to do this two or three times, but if all goes well the effect of the steam will be to draw the egg out.

Sometimes, even with this drastic treatment, the hen will still need your help, and so you very gently assist her to manipulate the egg by lightly pressing on the egg with your thumb and fore-finger from the outsider, usually after steam has been used. Even if the egg has not been passed, the steam will have had a loosening effect on the muscles of the hen, and with your help she should pass the egg. Great care must be taken to apply only light pressure as any likelihood of breaking the egg inside the hen should be avoided at all costs.

I have known occasions when a very severely egg-bound hen has eventually passed the egg, and as this has happened so the vent has completely opened and the cloaca (the inside of the vent) has protruded and become exposed. Should this happen do not be alarmed, just gently push the protrusion back into place. In a second the vent will look its normal shape. A little petroleum jelly smoothed over this area will help to relieve the soreness.

Most hens that experience egg-binding often look sick even when the egg is laid, but I have had hens that have had this disorder which I felt could not live owing to the severe strain they have had before they could lay their egg; and yet in a few days they have appeared quite fit again. Of course, you would not use them again for breeding that season.

The steam treatment for egg-binding should only be used as a very last resort. I have described this treatment only for the reason that at times you might have a severely egg-bound hen which without extreme help would die anyway. Then and only then would I suggest you resort to steam.

We should help to prevent this ailment by seeing our stock always has plenty of cuttle-fish bone and grit available.

Lastly, do not think that egg-binding is a common occurrence in budgies. This is not so. I know of fanciers who have kept these delightful birds for years and have never had one egg-bound.

WHEN YOUR BIRD SLEEPS ON ONE LEG

I am referring to this as many owners think there is something wrong when they notice their pet asleep with only one leg on the perch. I am pleased to reassure them that this is not so. On the contrary, it is a sign that all is well.

When a bird sleeps like this it is well and sure of itself, therefore it finds it more relaxing to sleep on one leg. On the other hand when it is off-colour and sick it is not so confident and grips the perch with both feet to make certain it does not fall off. So when a budgie is resting on one leg it is an indication that it is really well.

TONICS

Having completed the list of ailments, I feel it would be appropriate here to mention tonics for budgies, as many owners ask me about this.

I have already mentioned millet sprays, which are very beneficial and a tit-bit that all budgies enjoy. From my experience millet sprays, plus chickweed (which is a weed found in many gardens) and seeding grasses when they are available, are all the tonics budgies require.

But when these two greenfoods are not available (such as in winter time) I have found rose hip syrup to be an excellent substitute for getting budgies into good condition.

This syrup should be given to budgies in a very diluted state. For pet birds two drops, given twice a week in the drinker filled with water should do nicely.

If you keep a number of budgies, one teaspoonful of syrup to a pint of water should be the mixture (after putting syrup in water thoroughly stir). When using rose-hip syrup, which can be obtained from any chemist, always wash out the container that you mix the syrup and water in and also the drinkers after they have been used, so that no sourness will occur.

I have mentioned the tonics I give my own birds, but there are many others.

Years ago cod-liver oil mixed with seed was used by virtually every budgerigar breeder, and although I don't think it is used quite so extensively today, there are still many who continue to do so. I would not recommend this for pet birds, as where only a little amount of seed is consumed each day, there is always the risk that seed mixed with cod-liver oil might be several days old before being given to the bird, therefore becoming rancid—with results perhaps disastrous to your pet. Years ago I used cod-liver oil with the seed, and by making sure that I never gave this to my birds when stale, never had any trouble, and usually my birds became in excellent condition.

For those of you who would like to try this oil as a conditioner for your birds, here are the details. Mix one teaspoonful of cod-liver oil to one pound of seed (if you have a large number of birds work out approximately how much seed they will eat in four days, say for instance it is ten pounds of seed add ten teaspoonfuls of this oil to it) and mix, stirring well with a spoon. Allow this to stand for twenty-four hours then feed to your birds. After using seed mixed with cod-liver oil for four days, throw out seed not used, and empty seed dishes or hoppers that contain seed mixed with cod-liver oil, wash and dry them out, and replenish them with seed which had been mixed with this oil twenty-four hours previously.

When I used to use cod-liver oil I found it beneficial to give it to my birds from September until the first chick hatched, I never gave it to breeding pairs which had young as I felt it might be too rich for the youngsters. I found cod-liver oil to be an excellent product for strengthening budgies before breeding, but now having tried rose-hip syrup with equally good results and, finding it easier to use, do not use cod-liver oil. But know of fanciers who swear this oil is the best.

Besides those tonics already mentioned, there are many other stimulants that can be obtained for budgies, such as yeast preparations and vitamin mineral supplements that can be sprinkled on the seed. Soluble tonics that can be added to the water. Protein food can be given dry and others need to be mixed with water. And so I could go on. There is no doubt that the budgie is certainly looked after by the commercial side of the bird food industry and the veterinary chemists. There is a wide range of tonics to choose from.

To conclude this chapter I would like to stress again that although budgies can suffer from any of the complaints I have mentioned, very, very few actually do. I have listed them purely as a duty, as from the outset of this book my one aim has been to assist and enlighten those who keep the wonderful budgie, or intend to do so.

It is surprising how many owners become really concerned about their bird's welfare. (I know this by the number of anxious owners I get at my home—not because I am a veterinary surgeon, but because they have learnt that I keep birds and feel I can advise them.) And I am pleased to say that on many occasions I have been able to reassure them that the symptoms that their bird has had such as regurgitation is in fact not a sign of illness but of health.

For this reason I have written fully about diseases and ailments, and hope that both the birds and their owners will benefit from the information I have given.

TEN

The Budgie as a Healer of the Sick

We all know how popular the budgie is as a pet, but very few realize how much healing effect this little bird can have on the lonely and distressed.

Speaking from actual experience, one budgie I gave to a boy was responsible for uniting him with his stepfather, who, until the intervention of the budgie, treated him more as an animal than as a human being. The boy had never heard this man say a kind word to him, and when he took the budgie I gave him he expected to suffer at the hands of his step-parent for doing so. In fact there was a 'storm' when he arrived home, but then master budgie took over. He got out of the cage and, after circling the room, decided for some reason to pitch on the stepfather's hand. As it attempted to do this the man waved his hands angrily to frighten the bird the same as he did to the rest of the household. However, the fear that the humans had of this man was not shared by our friend the budgie, and, after flying around, again decided to land on the stepfather's hand. The boy said he stood petrified, being afraid that the man would really hurt it, as he was in a temper. Then the miracle happened, the bird landed on his hand, and instead of frightening it, the stepfather started to talk and said what a lovely bird it was. Neither the boy nor his mother could believe it! From that moment things changed, the hard bitter man who appeared to hate everyone became kind and considerate and wanted everyone who came to the house to see 'his' bird. For some reason the two became inseparable.

This is a true story and is remarkable, as a young budgie accomplished in a few minutes a change in character that no human being could have achieved. The stepson to whom I originally gave the bird said he did not have much to do with it as the stepfather looked upon it as his own property, but the boy did not mind, as from that day he was living with a happy step-parent and not a tyrant as before.

I have also known of budgies which have achieved wonderful 'cures' for the owner's loneliness or nerves. These conditions are often caused by people being on their own most of the time without someone to talk to, and in cases like these the budgie is the complete 'rescuer'. If there is one thing this little feathered friend likes more than anything else it is to be talked to, and once a budgie is installed as a pal often remarkable results occur. So if any of you are lonely and your spirits are low a budgie could be your cure.

I am often asked, "Can you let me have a young budgie, poor old Mrs. Smith who lives near me is sad these days since her husband died?" Or this, "Have you any young budgies, my gran is very run down and the doctor says she should have a bird for company?" If I have none to spare myself I usually manage to get one from one of the other fanciers, and my good deed is done! In most cases it is truly remarkable what the company of a budgie can achieve, and it is only on very rare occasions that the owners do not benefit in some way.

What makes the budgie an ideal pet is that in addition to its wonderful personality, it is inexpensive to keep. It should cost about 15 pence per week to provide the requirements for one bird. It is clean in its habits, and it is not necessary to clean its cage more than once every four or five days, unless you wish to do it more often.

So if any of you feel the need for company, or know of someone who has got the feeling that there is nothing to live for (this feeling is much more common than is generally imagined) the solution could be a budgie. Many people I know have felt that there is something to live for after all, once they have their feathered friend.

I have written this chapter as a tribute to the budgie and the wonderful comfort he or she often gives to the sick and sad. I have bred budgies, exhibited them, and trained them to talk, but nothing has given me more pleasure than to let a lonely person have one of my birds, and to see how happy that person has become within a short while of having it.

ELEVEN

Why I Love the Budgie

This is one chapter that need not necessarily have been written, as from what you have already read, you cannot but realize the great fondness I have for the budgie. And yet I have decided to write it because to me the budgie, out of all birds, is 'different'. Having kept various cage birds as well as pigeons and poultry, I have learnt the virtues that these various species have, and still have a liking for them. Despite this, of them all the budgie has that 'something' which the others haven't. I know that fanciers who keep other varieties of birds will not agree with me, but this is my book, with my personal feelings in it, and that is how I feel!

Many people all over the world keep budgies purely because of the many colours that they can be obtained in, and when you realize that there are over 100 colours or combination of colours in budgies, you can fully understand how they are fascinated by them. I too like to see the numerous colours of the budgie, but this is not the reason they captivate me. The reason for my liking this bird is its intelligence and personality. I honestly don't think there is another species of bird which varies so much and in so many ways as the budgie. If you study them as I do, you will find that every one has his or her own personality. There is nothing sheep-like in the budgie, each one is an individual with a separate character. As with humans there are those with good points, and others with bad ones, but to me that is life, and makes the keeping of these little parakeets interesting—and, yes, at times frustrating—but never boring.

Perhaps you are wondering whether budgies really differ from other birds. To see this, just imagine human behaviour, and from the following you will see that the budgie is almost human in manner. First take the jealous type in humans. Budgies have their counterpart, the jealous hen, for instance, who really loves her mate. She is most gentle and loving to him but 'watch out the young lady who tries to flirt with him', she's soon shown where to 'get-off' as far as Mrs. Budgie is concerned Her 'husband is her's for keeps whether he likes it or not, so any other female had better keep out of her way or else.

Then we have the unfaithful one. Oh yes, he has his partner, but who nicer to go with than the lady in the next cage if there's a chance the missis is busy in the nest-box?

Another character often in an aviary is the bully. Nobody really likes big-head, but he is a strong looking chap, all the girls seem to adore him, and he's so strong that he rules the roost—so, as with humans, the only way to have peace in the house is to let the bully have his own way and the best of everything. If the bully is in with all the other birds in one breeding pen, which is known as colony breeding, that will often mean he gets someone else's wife as well at least for a short while. When for instance the bully took 'Mr. Humble's' beloved wife poor 'Humble' was heartbroken for a few days. Then a 'younger bit of stuff' was put in the aviary and immediately the bully started chasing her round the place like a greyhound.

He soon forgot 'Mrs. Humble' ever existed. True, 'Mrs. Humble' had been unfaithful, but her husband was a forgiving sort and she was soon back with him. It was a case of forgive and forget.

You can see by what I have just written, even though in a fanciful way, that budgies can and do act in very similar ways to humans. I have just shown you what could be classed as their bad points. Here are some of a different nature. First, the devoted mother. I have at present in my birdroom just such a hen. She is only two years old now. Last year she reared seven youngsters from two nests. This is nothing remarkable, but she would have reared more had I let her. However, it was only a month or so ago that I really learned how devoted a mother she was. I had been feeding the birds, and I decided to look in the nest boxes to see all was well, I looked in the cage first and there was no cock bird there. This was not unusual because the cock bird mated to the devoted mother I am now writing about often went into the nest-box to feed her. I opened the door of the nest-box and there was the cock bird, dead. It was lying on top of the two babies which were about two weeks old, by the look of the bird he had been dead several hours, I removed it, and had a look at the babies. Despite the fact that her mate had been lying dead in the box for sometime, the hen had still fed the youngsters to the full as their crop's were bulging. I left the bird-room wondering if I had done right in leaving the chicks with their mother instead of fostering them out to other nests. I thought that perhaps, once she realized that her mate was missing, she might neglect them, but I needn't have worried as she never left the nest except to relieve herself and feed. I am pleased to say the two youngsters are now just old enough to feed themselves and healthy birds they are.

Besides devoted mothers like the one I have just mentioned, there are other hens who besides feeding their own chicks will often take a waif and stray because for some reason he or she is unwanted by its own parents.

No two budgies are completely the same. Even among brothers and sisters there are the gentle and the cruel, the placid ones and the nervy ones, those that like company and those who like to stay on their own. Naturally I am now referring to those kept in aviaries; but even the single pet will have its own personality, and the new owner need only have it a day or so to know what sort it is.

To conclude, you can see that those who decide to keep budgies and take the trouble to study them as individuals receive a great sense of purpose in this. The owner who looks upon every bird as being the same (and many do) is missing one of the great pleasures of the fancy.

TWELVE

The Budgerigar Society and Further Books on the Budgerigar

In this final chapter I am including some more details and information, which I hope will acquaint the reader even further with the budgerigar fancy. First there is:

The Budgerigar Society,
Secretary, A. R. Secombes,
57 Stephyns Chambers,
Bank Court,
Marlowes,
Hemel Hempstead, Hertfordshire.

From time to time I have referred to this society, which has developed and nurtured the budgerigar fancy in all its aspects. It is probably the finest live-stock Association in the world, and the envy of many who would like to emulate it. It provides guidance to anyone who needs it.

Each of its members is issued with a code number. This code number is engraved on the rings which the member obtains from the society, the official closed rings for putting on budgies' legs, thus ensuring the identity of the breeder.

The Budgerigar Society also helps many budgerigar associations in their shows, in the way of providing rosettes, diplomas, trophies, spoons, and cash special prizes through their Ring Prize scheme. Its various committees represent every part of Great Britain, and it also gives guidance to overseas associations. Among its many activities it promotes its own championship show, which is the world's largest exhibition of budgerigars.

Here, with the Society's kind permission, are extracts from its Handbook of Rules.

GENERAL RULES

Objects—The objects of the Society are:

(*a*) To promote the breeding and development of the Budgerigar in all parts of the world.
(*b*) To protect the interests of breeders and exhibitors.
(*c*) To assist the progress of scientific knowledge.
(*d*) To facilitate the exchange of ideas by the publication of a *Bulletin* covering the Society's field of work.
(*e*) To support the exhibition of budgerigars by granting patronage to shows and assisting them in other ways.
(*f*) To reward work of outstanding merit with prizes or other marks of recognition.
(*g*) To interest the public generally in the objects and activities of the Society.
(*h*) To assist and work in unison with the area societies and all clubs at home and abroad catering for the budgerigar.
(*i*) To serve as the parent body in a closely-knit international organisation.

Subscription—In previous editions I have quoted the current subscription charges for membership of the Budgerigar Society both for fanciers in Britain and those who reside overseas, but due to the constant fluctuation in currency valuation throughout the world, to do so now would be misleading.

Therefore I would suggest that any reader who would like these details should contact the General Secretary, The Budgerigar Society, whose address is on page 109.

Each member will have a vote at the annual election of B.S. representatives to the General Council. Age of junior members: minimum 7 years up to 16 years. Closed coded rings shall be issued only to members whose subscriptions have been paid and on the official ring form.

The General Council may in its absolute discretion accept or reject applications for membership or applications for affiliation or re-affiliation, without assigning any reason.

At budgerigar shows there are junior, beginner, novice, intermediate, and champion sections. Juniors normally compete in their own section until they are over sixteen, when they go into the beginner section. Adults usually commence exhibiting in the beginner section, going through each section in turn until they eventually qualify as champion exhibitors.

For further guidance here is the Budgerigar Society's definition of junior, beginner, novice and intermediate.

Junior—A junior paying a juvenile subscription must exhibit in junior classes only but the best junior bird should be judged along with other birds for the best in show. In the case of championship shows it must first compete for best of its colour.

Beginner—A beginner may exhibit in beginners' classes for two show seasons, or until he or she has won four first prizes in beginner section in full classes in competition at open shows, whichever is the longer period.

Novice—A novice may exhibit in novice classes for three show seasons, or until he or she has won four first prizes in novice section in full classes in competition at open shows, whichever is the longer period.

Intermediate—An intermediate may exhibit in intermediate classes for four show seasons, or until he or she has won six first prizes in intermediate section in full classes in competition at open shows, whichever is the longer period.

Note I—A full class shall be seven exhibits with not less than three exhibitors.

Note II—A member who commences the season as a beginner, a novice or an intermediate may continue as such until the end of that show season, even if he or she has attained a higher status.

Note III—Breeders' classes and any age classes at open shows are considered 'OPEN' competition for the purpose of the above definitions.

For those of you who have budgies, and are considering exhibiting them and would like to make your own show cages here is the specification of The Budgerigar

Society standard show cage *(Incorporating Patent No. 755106)*:

SPECIFICATION

SIZE—overall measurements: 14 in. long, 12 in. high, 6½ in. wide.

WOOD—top and bottom, ¼ in. finish; sides and false roof, 5/16 in. finish; in red or white deal, pine or redwood. Back good 4 mm. plywood nailed outside.

DOOR—(*a*) size: 4 in. by 3½ in.; (*b*) fasteners: one flat loop wire, 15 gauge, length 1½ in. outside, 1¼ in. inside, at bottom left-hand of door, ¾ in. from left edge and ¾ in. from bottom edge. One plain brass desk turn, 1 in. long fixed above top left-hand door in line with the loop wire fastener; (*c*) two strong brass hinges, 1 in. by ⅝ in. (when open) at right-hand side, fixed ⅜ in. from top and bottom respectively; (*d*) to open ⅞ in. wire S-hook, 16 gauge, in centre of door; (*e*) left-hand edge, top and bottom of door, sloping bevel cut; right-hand edge straight cut (to take hinges); 3¾ in. overall from cage bottom, and centred with sides.

FRONT RAIL—(*a*) height 2¾ in. from cage floor, (*b*) thickness of wood 5/16 in. finish; (*c*) pot fixed on removable door, 3⅜ in. by ¾ in. sloping bevel cut; (*d*) door pull, ⅝ in. wire S-hook, 16 gauge.

DRINKER—white plastic, 2½ in. by 1½ in. with ¼ in. flange at each end and ⅝ in. deep.

PERCHES—(*a*) length 4½ in. overall, diameter 9/16 in. finished; ends flush cut, not pointed or cone-shaped; (*b*) plain boss at back projecting ½ in. diameter 1¼ in., not painted; (*c*) position: screw holes at back of cage to be 5½ in. from the bottom, overall, and, 4⅜ in. apart; perches at front then centre with the crossbar.

WIRE FRONT—(*a*) comprises 21 wires, 14 gauge, mesh ⅝ in. centre to centre; (*b*) height of crossbar, 5½ in. overall, *i.e.* including bottom of cage; (*c*) for strength, double-punched, set ⅜ in. apart; (*d*) curve at top, ¾ in. bow; (*e*) fixing, three wires left as spikes at top and bottom.

TOP—(*a*) width approximately 5½ in. sufficiently wide to cover strengthening bar; (*b*) hand hole, kidney-shaped, 3¼ in. by 1¼ in.; (*c*) height of sloping false roof, 8½ in. from floor of cage.

COLOUR—inside and wire front, white; outside, black.

NAME—no maker's name or mark must appear on the cage.

Note—As from MAY 1971 judges were instructed to disqualify birds shown in WELDED FRONT cages.

It should be borne in mind that show cages besides conforming to the above specification must also have the white ivorine (Budgerigar Society Patent) plate on the front rail, as shown on the standard show cage illustrated elsewhere. These ivorine plates are obtainable from the Budgerigar Society. A budgie exhibited in a standard show cage without this plate would be disqualified.

Area Societies Affiliated to the Budgerigar Society

These societies recognize the Budgerigar Society as the parent body, and each send two delegates to represent them at the General Council Meetings of the Budgerigar Society which are held at regular intervals, so keeping in touch with all Budgerigar Society matters and decisions.

The area societies also do much useful work within their area boundaries. They issue their own members with their own area code number, so that if a member of an area society is not also a member of the Budgerigar Society he can still obtain the official closed ring for putting on his or her bird's leg through the area society. Needless to say an exhibitor who is not a member of the Budgerigar Society would not be allowed to win this Society's own Special Prizes which are for Budgerigar Society members only. Naturally many exhibitors belong to both societies. The area societies give guidance and advice, they grant patronage to most shows in their area, and like the Budgerigar Society have their own panel of judges, have their club shows, and publish bulletins and a year book.

For a small fee any association in the area can become affiliated to the area society. These Associations, some with hundreds of members, some with very few, are asked by the area society to which they are affiliated to send two representatives to their meetings, which like those of the Budgerigar Society are held regularly.

All this shows how remarkably organized the budgerigar fancy is. From the Budgerigar Society we go to the affiliated Area Societies, and then to the individual Associations who are affiliated to the Area Societies, each in turn inter-knit one into the other. Understandably this is considered the finest organized fancy in the world.

The British area societies affiliated to the Budgerigar Society are:

Lancashire, Cheshire and North Wales (including the Isle of Man) Budgerigar Society
Lincolnshire and East Anglia Budgerigar and Foreign Bird Society
London and Southern Counties Budgerigar Society
Midland Budgerigar and Foreign Bird Association
Northern Budgerigar Society
The Scottish Budgerigar Society
South Midland Budgerigar Society
South Wales and Monmouthshire Budgerigar Society
Western Counties Budgerigar and Foreign Bird Society
Yorkshire Budgerigar Society

Advice for Juveniles

During the recent years there has been a substantial increase in the number of young people who keep budgies (or other cage birds for that matter) and quite rightly the societies which cater for these birds have formed junior sections for their young members, who are under sixteen years of age.

If you keep budgies and are 16 or under but have never joined an association, the following details are for you.

The Budgerigar Society will welcome you as a junior member if you are between 7 and 16 years of age. If you join you will enjoy most of the privileges of the society as well as receiving their bulletins and year book with your name and code number in it as one of their paid up members.

You may also join your area society affiliated to the Budgerigar Society, the subscription to be a member of one of these now varies in each area, and often changes yearly. You can get the details of the subscription and the address of your area society's secretary from the Budgerigar Society. But if you write to them please enclose a stamped addressed envelope. If you become a member of an area society this will provide you with more bulletins and a handbook and the chance to win the area society's Special Prizes at the shows.

Naturally if you want to enjoy your hobby to the full you should join at least one local budgerigar or cage bird society so that you can attend their meetings, help at their shows, show your birds there and generally enjoy the pleasure of other fanciers' company. Subscriptions for membership of local clubs are usually very moderate—in my own town they vary from 15 new pence, to 25 new pence for a yearly subscription.

If you wish to know the address of your local or nearest club the Citizens Advice Bureau in your nearest town will advise you.

Lastly there is one club which is purely for young people who are interested in birds. This is the Junior Bird League which is sponsored by the weekly cage bird journal *Cage and Aviary Birds* which is published each Thursday. You only have to pay once to become a member of this league and the subscription is 50 new pence. For this you get a very nice badge and a certificate.

Being a member of the Junior Bird League entitles you to allow your birds to compete for the attractive Junior Bird League Diplomas which this league donates to most bird shows. It also entitles you to a cheaper admission price to the magnificent National Exhibition of Cage Birds. And lastly if you have any interesting stories or pictures of birds the Junior Bird League will consider publishing them on their own page in *Cage and Aviary Birds*.

The address of this league if you wish to write to them is:

The Secretary,
Junior Bird League,
Surrey House,
Throwley Way,
Sutton, Surrey, SM1 4QQ

Further books on the Budgerigar

Having read this book, perhaps you feel that you would like to know even more about budgerigars.

Should this be so, there are several books about them. But I am going to mention three which I have found to be particularly helpful, and comparatively easy to understand.

The first is beyond question the finest text-book ever written on the budgerigar it is *The Cult of The Budgerigar* by W. J. Watmough which deals fully with all aspects of the fancy. It is excellently illustrated and has some wonderful colour plates depicting what the various coloured varieties of budgies look like. Yes! it is a wonderful book in every sense of the word.

Another book I have found useful is *Budgerigars And How To Breed Them* by C. H. Rogers. Although a small, and modestly priced, book, it has much useful detail and makes most interesting reading.

The third book is for the budgerigar fancier who really wants to study the colour genetics of these birds it is *Budgerigar Matings and Colour Expectations* which is published by the Budgerigar Society of England. This manual which contains the original tables of colour expectations in budgerigars by the famous German geneticist, Dr. H. Duncker, has been brought up to date by two English fanciers F. S. Elliott and E. W. Brooks who laboured many years at this work.

This remarkable book is the most comprehensive ever published on colour genetics in budgerigars. It includes details of 1,830 possible matings, and at first glance appears very complex, but once the basic code for finding matings are understood, it is reasonably easy to follow, and details of any particular mating can usually be found in a minute or so.

This book which costs about 60 new pence, or 2 dollars, is an invaluable guide for all serious breeders of budgerigars, and one they should own in their own interest.

INDEX

INDEX

Advice for juveniles, 114–16
Affiliated Area Societies, 113–14
Ailments, 78–101
Albinos, 39, 48, 61, 71
Anatomy of Budgerigar, 75
Apples, 23
Asthma, 86–8

Back skull, 75
Barheads, 39
Bathing, 51–2
Beaks, 75, 88–90
Bleeding, 82–83
Books, 116–117
Breeding, 32–39
Breeding cages, 32–3, 79
Breeding stock, 34–5
Budgerigar Society, 41–2, 109–114
  Exhibition colour standards, 63–77
  Exhibitor status rules, 111
  General rules, 110
  Ideal Bird, 48, 59–60

Cabbage, 23
Cage and Aviary Birds paper, 115–116
Cere, 12–13, 75
Cheek-patches, 75
Chickweed, 23
Chills, 88
Cinnamons, 44–8, 61, 65–7
Claws, 88–90
Clearwings, 61, 69–70
Cloaca, 97
Closed coded rings, 53–6
Cod-liver oil, 99–100
Colony breeding, 106
Colour descriptions, 43–5, 63–77
Colour, scale of points, 61–2
Colour genetics, 45–9
Concave, 37
Constipation, 81–2
Control (cage) breeding, 79
Crown, 75
Cuttle-fish bone, 22

Dark-eyed clears, 62, 74
Dark-green, 61, 63
Dominant pied, 62, 72–3
Draughts, 57

Egg-binding, 95–8
Eggs, 37

Encouraging to eat, 87
Enteritis, acute, 91–3
Exhibiting in breeder classes, 53
Exhibiting, prizes and comments, 58–9
Expectations, colour, 47–9
Eye, 75

Fallows, 61, 70–1
Feeding, 19–23
Feet, 75
Flight, cages, 33
Flight, feathers, 75
Food mastication, 21
French moult, 13–14
Frontal, 75
Front-line, 75

Genetics, 45–9
Grass, 23
Greenfood, 23
Gregariousness, 33
Grey, 45, 61, 64
Greygreen, 45, 61, 63
Greywings, 61, 67–8
Grit, 21–2
Growths, 85

History of the budgie, 40–2
Hens, sexing of, 12–13

Ideal Budgerigar, 48, 59–60
  Scale of points, 61–2
Injuries, 78–101
Instruments, 32
Irritation due to lice, 85–6

John Gould (Explorer), 40–1
Junior Bird League, 116

Lacewings, 62, 77
Legs, 75
Lettuce, 23
Lice, 85–6
Light-green, 61–3
Lumps, 85
Lutinos, 39, 48, 61, 71

Mask, 75
Mating tables, 47–9
Mauve, 45, 61, 64
Millet-sprays, 20

Nest-box, 36–7, 79
Night-blindness, 84
Night-fright, 83–4

Obesity, 94–5
Olive-green, 45, 61, 63
Olive-yellow, 61, 63
Opaline, 44, 48–9, 61–2, 64–6
Outside flight, 96

Perches, 24–8
Perpetual spinach, 23
Pet cages, 26–7
Pied, Clear-flighted, 62, 73–4
  Dominant, 62, 72–3
  Recessive, 62, 76
Principal points of a budgerigar 75
Prize money, 58–9

Purchasing a budgie, 13–17
Purchasing breeding stock, 34–5

Rainbow, 44
Recessive pied, 62, 76
Regurgitation, 93
Ringing budgies, 38, 53–6
Rose-hip syrup, 98–100
Rump, 75

Scaly-face, 78–80
Seed, 19–21
Seeding grasses, 23
Sexing budgies, 12–13
Sex, linkage, 48–9
Shoulders, 75
Show cage specification, 112
Skin, injury, 84–5
Skyblue, 61, 63
Sleeping on one leg, 98
Soft-moult, 56–7
Sprains, 80–1
Stomach upsets, 90–1

Talking, training, 29–31
Temperature, harmful fluctuation of, 57
Tit-bits, 22
Tonics, 98–101
Travelling Case, 32

Vent, 75, 81
Vent, oiling, 96
Violet, 61, 64

Water, 18
Wattle, 75
Wheezing, 86–8
White, suffused, 61, 64
Whitewings, 61, 70
Wild budgies, 43
Wings, 75

Yellow-face blue, 44, 62, 71
Yellow-wing greens, 61, 69–70
Yellows, 61, 63
Young barhead budgies, 39, 80